DING DONG BELL

(And Other Irreverent Teachings)

By
SANDRA L. DUDLEY

A division of Squire Publishers, Inc.
4500 College Blvd.
Leawood, KS 66211
1/888/888-7696

Copyright 2001
Printed in the United States

ISBN: 1-58597-112-X

Library of Congress Control Number: 2001096818

A division of Squire Publishers, Inc.
4500 College Blvd.
Leawood, KS 66211
1/888/888-7696

Dedicated to

Ban and Papa

who were a part of that

"Greatest Generation"

and who nourished and nurtured

three more generations of our family

ACKNOWLEDGMENTS

Names and places in this novella have been changed to conceal further complicity or controversy. I wrote this manuscript in 1983-84 while waiting for a teaching job, and upon completion, and with the advent of a new job in 1985, I buried the script in a file box for sixteen years. Only when I retired in 2000 did I return to that story and to a newfound appreciation of what I had documented.

I wish to thank my three children, Derek, Rama and Dale, for their unconditional love and support as they have watched my life ebb and flow through the years with commitments to family, athletics and education. Were they not steadfast in unaltered faith and devotion, I could not dare to dream.

INTRODUCTION

When Lamar Alexander was Secretary of Education, he said, "We are talking about a revolution in education. It is a moment in time when you interrupt what you're doing and ask the most fundamental questions: what kind of people are we? what is important to us? and what do we have to contribute to the place where we live?" He expressed the opinion that the problems of education needed to be faced "community by community."

A decade later, though, we have added to our many challenges facing education. It is often an unspoken, secret-society understanding in a small, homogeneous community that to "speak out" is to "move out." As a result, no one is encouraged to take an adversarial position less one suffers the role of not being a "team player." This coaching, anvil-hammer mentality has long resulted in a capitulation to inertia when at a most crucial time in education and worldwide political climate, people are feeling a need to no longer accept a supplicant role to prescribed, programmed thinking. We need to be asking, "For whom does the school bell toll?"

When a parent complains that Dick and Jane graduated from high school without an adequate background in academia necessary to compete in larger universities, I cannot empathize with this unsubstantial criticism. Rather instead, my first question would be to a good number of parents and school systems: what are your priorities?

From school systems with a population of two hundred to school systems of two thousand and more, I never seem to hear an inquiry as to what are the priorities. Therefore, we continue to imitate a society which gives assent to the prominence of athletics over academics. We refuse to acknowledge this, but we choose to cloak the emphasis, both locally and nationally, under the guise of building character. Here in the Midwest in schools of populations of about five to six hundred pupils within a high school, one can safely estimate that there is approximately one coach for every eight players on a football team, not to mention additional student trainers and helpers.

The harsh realities, whether we find alternating statistics or not, is that in our secondary schools we have evolved from a system which hired teachers and hoped they could coach to a system which now hires coaches and hopes that they can teach. For example, when I was looking for a job at age fifty-two, I was asked if I could teach English and be assistant girls' tennis coach in the fall and assistant boys' tennis coach in the spring? Would that have been asked of an English teacher prior to the '60s? How, then, can we expect to change the various troubled areas of parenting, teaching, financing and administering until we will first clearly postulate what is at the root of all of our degenerative, pejorative school systems, and that is PRIORITIES. Once we articulate a clear focus on whether we consider reading, writing and arithmetic as at least twice as important as athletics, instead of being equal or less, we will deserve the education we have.

Studies show that in Europe one out of five in education are administrators, and two out of five are administrators in America. Isn't that such a revealing, telling order of priorities? Is it even necessary to allocate expenditures to investigate causes as to our unproductive, failing results in education? Time and time again, I have gone to minuscule meetings that extol the virtues and importance of our teachers as the very essence and backbone of education, and after the meeting is over, we see a return to the little ant hills of busy people with titular positions (and paychecks equaling $15,000 to $20,000 larger than any faculty member) and with paper loads of policies they carry from one ant hill to another; and meanwhile, Sisyphus (the teacher) is still trying to roll the boulder up the mountain day by day.

We need to decide whether moving a boulder (teaching) every day is significantly more important, in terms of comparative worth, than titles! If we have twice as many titled people in our school system in America than in Europe, we need to examine how the distributions of the taxpayers' dollars can not only be effective but also be justified. We teachers will accept gratuity for trips to seminars to distant shores as long as money is available. In the process, yes, we meet people; yes, the accommodations are luxurious (for the most part); yes, the food is plentiful; and yes, the dance band is great. Add a tryst to all of this, and a few will conclude that the conference was an overall success. The bottom line, though, is that I do not want to spend MY money for something where I feel I could just as easily have read the book instead or seen the videotape for a fraction of the cost. I believe that the taxpayer shares the same sentiment, and I believe that the day has arrived when excruciating decisions are necessary to explain the nexus of concern for budget allocations.

Perhaps there will be a mighty Zeus somewhere on Mt. Olympus who will see the task of reaffirmation and rededication as not Herculean but as American and will, therefore, declare we can first start with priorities in education. Once that happens, we may find that numerous pebbles of poor judgment and poor choices in education today will be easier to bear than boulders. What kind of people are we? What is important to us? Who will ring the Ding Dong Bell?

DING DONG BELL

Ding dong bell,
Pussy's in the well.
Who put her in?
Little Johnny Green.
Who pulled her out?
Little Tommy Stout.
What a naughty boy was that,
To try to drown poor pussy cat
Who never did any harm
and killed the mice in his father's barn.

"It is said that when one gives something away to help another, that it will return many times over. Call this $100 a gift, an investment, just a small acknowledgment to one who has done so much for so many, this writer not withstanding. Go buy that typewriter and write! You sent me this card a while back. I return it to you with a little something that I found in my bedroom one morning. Keep the faith and the spirit …"

Love,
Stan

And, thus, I began my book.

Direction A: The plural of nouns ending in "y" following a consonant is formed by changing "y" to "i" and adding "es."

Direction B: The plural of nouns ending in "o" preceded by a vowel is formed by adding "s."

If it bothers you that the above directions state "following" in Direction A and "preceded" in Direction B, then read the last part of this book first, and the first part of this book last.

"I AM ONE OF THE LEADING AUTHORITIES on William Faulkner in the Midwest. I expect you, as students, to become acquainted with the procedures of scholarly research into the writings of William Faulkner and to acquire an appreciation of the genius of an American writer. His work is prodigious to American Literature. I will expect you to examine, most thoroughly, a small portion of this prolific literary output so that you will understand and recognize why this brilliant Southern writer was worthy of the Nobel Prize for Literature in 1950. I expect the very best from you the entire semester, and in every assignment."

Bull!! He expects this. He expects that. Does he ever think of asking what WE might expect out of him? I believe that if William Faulkner could see and hear how this English Department Chairman was teaching his class in the study of his writings, Faulkner would rise from his grave and vow never to take another drink in the hereafter or wherever. Of all the authors on God's literary roster to limit to clinical study, I tend to believe that Faulkner would be the last author to want his writings galvanized into sterile dissection. Pedantics and pedagogues have an approach to literature that stifles the very cores of creative expression. It seems that I have known teachers like this all my life, and I should be used to it by now, but then he is my teacher (and my boss), and so I should just learn to be reverent of the situation. Shouldn't I? Anyway, I will start at the beginning of what has been half a lifetime of irreverence as a student and a teacher.

1982

I was scanning the room looking for a fellow English-student friend while all of the sixty-some graduate students were being introduced by various dignitaries and department chairpersons. What I needed and prayed for in the English Department would be someone similar to my situation. In other words, I needed a forty-eight-year-old woman friend, preferably single, or divorced, like myself, who would be interested in an occasional show, dinner and insouciant conversation. I scanned the room for these same attributes in the opposite sex. All of Jill Clayborgh's movies made predicaments like mine seem so easy. In the movies, the right guy comes along, the right job and the right amount of money for enjoyable, desirous, glamorous living. In my case, I had had to borrow $3,000 from my folks until the 50-50 divorce settlement; I was earning $400 a month as graduate English assistant and paying $175 a month in rent — I was by no means a gal who could rely on beauty and charm to produce the "A" grades from the male teachers!

By the time we got to our individual departmental meetings, I could pretty well size up my colleagues for the coming year. No doubt our selection was based on the quid-pro-quo, for out of the ten assistants there was one black, one economically deprived, two ex-hippies, one cheerleader, one foreign student, one radical, one "old lady" (age 60), one middle-age woman (myself, age 48), and, oh yes, the boss' girlfriend. It had all the makings of an interesting beginning.

1942

Mom took me to school the very first day. Before the first-day enrollment though, Mom took my sister (two years older than I) up to the "dime store" to purchase all of our supplies and books. During those years of the 1940s, the dime store stocked all of the required texts for each grade, one through twelve. We always anxiously awaited the posting of the required texts in late August, several weeks before school started the day after Labor Day, and then with great excitement and anticipation, we headed for Ben Franklins or Kresses (the two dime stores in town) for what would be several hours of school shopping. A saleslady in the book department would take our lists and select either new or used books, whichever people could afford, and in the '40s most relied upon hand-me-down books as well as clothes. The fun part, though, was to buy our supplies like the Big Chief tablets, scissors, paste, erasers, rulers, and later in our advanced schooling, the ink pens and the zipper notebooks. I was always fascinated with taking my supplies back home where I could literally fondle the books and smell the new tablets. Sometimes, especially when we reached the junior high to senior high years, we were able to buy a new briefcase to carry all our books in, so we eagerly awaited the new styles, shapes and colors in briefcases. The earliest cases (during the grade-school years) were plaid colors of fabrics with flaps and buckles to hold everything in. When we were ready to graduate from the sixth grade, we looked forward to graduating from the fabric notebook to the "zipper" notebook with our names printed in gold on the front. Selecting the right notebook was as important to me as selecting the first automobile was to a teenage driver. Before school started, I arranged and rearranged my supplies from one place to another in my room, and I held my pencils in awe of the power that they could give me. From those earliest years of "getting ready" for school, I had a lasting, coveting love for the ownership of books and supplies.

  Even today, every time September arrives and I hear Walter Huston's version of "September Song," I have this primeval instinct to go purchase pens and notebooks. During the years between being a student and raising children, I was mesmerized by school supplies and the climate of overall expectancy that a new school year brings, but when it came time to begin my first day at school in the first grade, I was afraid to go to school, so my mom had to take me by the hand to school and stay in the room with me until she was sure I would not cry when she left. (Sociologists could no doubt explain this to us in terms of our being in an era where we were less sophisticated, less worldly or traveled, and less mobile than we are now.) Mothers at school the first day were quite common then. After all, most mothers had been home with us twenty-four hours of the day up to school age, and it was no easy transition for moms and kids to go from home to the unfamiliar environment of a school. Just knowing my mother was there beside me was all the explanation I needed to overcome shyness and doubt, and I managed not to cry (unlike many others) about the strangeness and newness of being among mostly strangers. That is, I managed not to cry about my shyness, but I did cry when the teacher was going down the aisle checking everyone's name and supplies. She was helping the boy in back of me, and when I turned to look at them, the teacher's elbow hit me right in the eye! That eye quickly produced tears, and thus began my first school years!

• • • • • • • •
1982
• • • • • • • •

Today, the noon-hour chimes on campus are playing "Claire De Lune." Southeast Kansas College was built in 1903 as the Southeast Kansas Manual Training School. The school's purpose was the special preparation of teachers of manual training and domestic science. The original school facilitated nineteen students and two teachers. From 1855 to 1860, the Kansas territorial legislature chartered eighteen universities and ten colleges, but only three of those schools survived, and two of the three (Manhattan and Lawrence) became state universities. By 1923, Southeast Kansas Manual Training School changed once again to Southeast Kansas College.

The architectural setting for the college is one of sedateness rather than superfluous pretensions. The buildings are a mixture of both old and new. Several buildings are old enough to be wrapped in ivy, and other newer buildings illustrate either the long, narrow glass windows or the large square-picture windows so characteristically reflecting contemporary architecture. Also, since the original campus was built on the one square block, the proximity of the buildings coincide with the convenience of small-town living. To students needing to exchange classes from one building to the next, the back doors of the buildings are equally essential as front doors, for like neighbors visiting their friends, there is an army of pedestrian traffic out of one back or front door to another building a short walk away. Pathways, along with sidewalks intersecting the square-block campus, serve as arteries pumping student movement from one vital area to another. At this college, students seldom hurry because of their nearness to classes, and so they exude an aura of relaxation and congeniality. There is no lack of space for walking, bicycling, talking, running, watching and resting. Before the 1960s, there was an abundance of solitude, and after the 1960s and early '70s, there resumed that habitual serenity and calm characteristic of peaceful, small-town living. About the only disruptive interruption in an otherwise orderly system in this college is when the grounds crew mow the campus lawn in early spring and fall, and even mowing has such a lulling lullaby to it that a student quite often lapses into either daydreaming or complete lack of consciousness. There are no classroom bells to signal the necessity of movement, as if the ringing noise is sacrilegious to the keeper of the tranquility. The chimes are the actual personality of the college, well within the hearing distance of students and personnel, clearly inviting loyalty and attention to the college one minute out of every hour of the day. The certainty of the sound of the chimes is a secure moment in one's day regardless of exterior influences upon one throughout the day.

  The Head of the Department called the meeting to order: "Welcome, graduate assistants. All of you have been selected because of your academic performance (pardon?) and honorably represent the department in teaching what I consider the most important course in the university: freshman composition. (Like hell — why do we have beginning teachers teaching it then?). What you can teach to our incoming freshmen will be skills and techniques that, hopefully, will make it possible for these students to communicate coherently and logically in written communications. Your advisor, Ms. Jan Burns, will be in charge of coordinating the freshman curriculum, and before I turn you over to her for your next meeting, we will now let you choose the hour each of you wishes to teach one class of freshman composition." The hands immediately go up to try to get the prime times for teaching class, such as 9:30, 10:30 or 11:30 a.m. or right after dinner. The boss' girlfriend's hand goes up, and she is chosen first (naturally). I take the unwanted and less popular hour of 8:30 a.m. because, believe it or not, I love the early morning hour when students are neither troublemakers, nor asleep, but not awake enough either so that a teacher can many times motivate and stimulate with only the slightest resistance from the students.

Once we were given our duty roster and "pep talk," we adjourned our meeting for the afternoon. It was still a warm summer day for August, so most of the ten GA's (graduate assistants) headed for a coke in the student union. I couldn't help but notice the older woman, Rebecca Norman, in front of me as we left the room. I had to hand it to her: she had herself quite "mod" looking. She had short, cropped, graying hair that she flipped back periodically with that superior aristocratic twist. Her clothes were definitely from elite shops, and she held a cigarette as if she were recently elected president of the cigarette sorority sisters. Well, anyway, we were lots closer to the same age than the "kids," so I gave it the old college try toward social amenities and asked: "Hey, Rebecca, how about going to the student union for a coke?"

"Sorry, Amy, I've got to meet Sandy and Jenny to find out what time we head back to Laneville. See you later."

"Sure, fine."

Like hell it was fine. Why couldn't she suggest my joining them, or she could have said, "How 'bout lunch tomorrow since I have made arrangements for today?" I made a mental note that man's best friend is his dog, and woman's *only* friend is her dog. I skipped the last meeting of the day — the tea and punch bit — and headed home to feed my dog. For the next twelve months, my life would pretty much be routine. I would be home to study by early afternoon, walk the dog before dark in order to keep her arthritis from settling in her joints, prepare for my one teaching class, and prepare for my three other enrolled classes I needed as part of the semester requirements for graduate assistants. Toward evening, I usually pulled the blinds, and I sat by myself thinking a lot about the unpredictable upheavals dominating my life.

• • • • • • • •
1944
• • • • • • • •

Our third grade teacher used to read to us every day about the Bobbsey Twins. None of the stories are familiar to youngsters now, of course, except that I can still close my eyes and visualize covered wagons in the fall-colored woods and see trails leading to glowing campfires where multi-colored gypsies sang and danced about in seemingly carefree lives to the eyes of the innocent. Every afternoon, I languidly entered that life while the kindly, soft-fleshed, rounded woman asked us to lay our heads on the desk as she began reading the serial episodes. For about an hour each afternoon, while the sun watched and warmed us through the walls of the south windows, I fantasized about adventures in nearby woods. Years later, undoubtedly as a positive, carryover influence upon my maturation, I relived, through my own children, the need for adventure by taking my three kids, neighbor kids, relatives, and even the dogs to the woods on weekends. We called it "exploring," and we went every weekend, weather allowing.

1982

My first day as a teacher in freshman composition and as a fellow graduate student had a rather propitious beginning. One of my better qualities is that I can truthfully lay claim to being organized and always on time. That can be an attribute under most all circumstances and a disadvantage only in the sense that once one is dressed, fed, bed made, house cleaned and dishes done, one has nothing to do but watch the clock until the proper time to leave. In that interim of waiting it out, one can get extremely nervous, and so naturally by the time I left for my 8:30 a.m. class, I had a slight toilet mishap from a bad case of first-day jitters, and I was set back approximately ten minutes — unheard of for me. That meant I needed to rush to stop for gas if I still wanted to be a half-hour early in my office. I self-helped myself at the gas station and went in to write out the check for the amount, only to be told NO CHECKS. I forgot I was in a college town! However, the attendant said that if I left security such as my billfold and driver's license, I could drive on and then return to pay him about noon, which would be between my dinner and my last class of the afternoon. Hence, I had lost another five minutes. That would give me twenty minutes to get ready for my freshman composition students. What would I say to them? How could I get off on the right foot? There was, of course, the choice of the professor's first-day lecture on materials, methods, grading and over-all teaching philosophy. And what was my philosophy? It seemed that I had taught most of my life, if not Bible school, tennis, swimming, then as a high school English teacher from 1972 to 1976. I should have had a teaching philosophy. The only thing was that it may not have been an appropriate philosophy for the first day of college. The department head would not approve if word got back to him, and it definitely showed irreverence for the English Department. Nevertheless, I would write on the board the order in which God created the university:

First Day: God created the Anthropology Department and gave us man and woman.
Second Day: God created the Psychology Department to analyze whether it was a man or woman.
Third Day: God gave man and woman the Music and Art Departments for spiritual nourishment.
Fourth Day: God created the History Department to record the accomplishments of man and woman.
Fifth Day: God created the Computer Department to catalog the records of the History Department.
Sixth Day: God created the Education Department to undo all of the above.
Seventh Day: On the seventh day, when it came time to create the English Department, God rested!

"As you can see, students, we have our work cut out for us this semester."

The rest of the lecture was basically "mainstream," and I delivered a much repeated opening philosophy that they would have more to learn from one another than they would have learned from me. I believe this, too. If I could shake them out of their preconceived, established prejudices, opinions and traditions and cause them to listen to their fellow classmates and to entertain new and open-minded ideas, I felt that I could have a successful class. Only by the end of the semester would I be able to tell if I had been successful in creating chemical reactions within the class. How students leave my class is more my objective than how they begin my class.

By the time I got back to the office, which I shared with three other graduate assistants, I could bask in the enjoyment of seeing the other graduate assistants fret about opening day. To add to my "lightened load" of having released my 8:30 a.m. teaching obligations for the first day, I also saw good news posted on our office door by the department secretary which said that our night class, taught by the Head of the Department, would not meet tonight.

"Why is that, Sharon?"

"They tell me he had to take a load of furniture down to his ex-wife in Florida," she said.

"Then, is it true that he did get a divorce?" I asked.

She nodded "Yes" and I responded with, "That's too bad — you know, with three kids and all." But she said nothing as if to contemplate, why is it too bad?

Obviously, I looked stumped by the exchange because as she proceeded down the hall, Mary Ann, the foreign student, added more information: "Amy, Sharon Hammons is a good friend of Connie Grimes and Connie is the boss' girlfriend. That's how things are around here."

"Okay, now I am putting together two and two, thanks." I thought about the department head — short, bald, beard, paunchy stomach — and thought the female population could breathe a sigh of relief to know he will be in someone else's bed by midnight and not preying on any other unsuspecting, innocent graduate assistants. "Any of the rest of you taking his course on Faulkner?"

"You won't be having that great sense of humor of yours after next week's class, Amy," James Boyd added.

About everyone else on the "Fourth Floor" went about their business of either teaching or taking classes except one — Leslie Adams, the cheerleader.

"What did James mean by that remark, Leslie?" I asked.

"Just that the head of the department is darn tough — I stay away from the man! Didn't anyone warn you?"

"No, I didn't know anyone to ask, and besides, I happen to like William Faulkner. I *want* to have the class."

"Then good luck, sweetie," Leslie offered. "You'll need it."

Hey, do I need worry, I ask myself? Didn't I just finish the summer with completing five of the required eight novels on the Faulkner seminar reading list? And am I not the one always to quote Lord Nelson: "I owe everything I have to being fifteen minutes beforehand." I don't need luck when I've got organization!!!

1943

I've never liked to believe that punishment is a deterrent to crime. Yet I think of the effective, successful policy of my second-grade, teacher-principal back in grade school. It was a well known fact that if a student were unfortunate enough to be sent to the principal's office for disciplinary reason, he or she was also going to be unfortunate enough to be subjected to the "rubber hose." The principal was an elderly, four-foot-four-one-hundred-pound woman who doubtfully looked no more capable of administering a ping-pong paddle, let alone a rubber hose! I never saw the rubber hose, nor did I know of anyone having been whipped, but the mere threat and intimidation of the rumors of the hose were a deterrent to suppress whatever incorrigible behavior I may have been tempted to nurture. That iron woman ruled, and ruled she did, over her orderly kingdom. I believe that I am correct in saying she was both feared and loved and thus remembered as a great administrator. That is why it is easy to understand why it is such a source of fulfillment, and pleasure, for me to go to my scrapbook of mementos and pull out my grade cards from that outstanding woman educator and be able to read her personal remarks to my parents:

First 9 weeks: Amy is a splendid pupil. Does lovely work for me.

Second 9 weeks: Amy seems very interested and happy with school.

Third 9 weeks: Amy is never idle. I wish I had a roomful of her.

Last 9 weeks: If every year in school is as pleasant for Amy as this one has been, she will be very fortunate.

This lady's accomplishments were unique to a generation unaccustomed to dictatorial, feminine leadership. This was an impressionable example to me in the formulation of teaching classroom discipline since I tend to adopt rather idealistic principles for hard-nose policy decisions. For the most part, I believe that if a person treats others with kindness and dignity, they will reciprocate with an equal equanimity of kindness and appreciation. What is difficult for me to accept is that this axiom does not always hold true in environments of alternative learning centers where students are isolated as punishment for failure to adhere to accepted behavioral standards. Give these students an inch and they will take a mile while simultaneously blaming either teacher or administrator for their fall from grace. Persecution, prejudice, and unfairness are built-in mechanisms for trouble in schools, and perhaps rightly so considering many of the backgrounds of the disciplinary students. That is why it often seems so contradictory to me that toughness, strictness, and objectivity is generally more necessary than a gesture of compassion and sympathy. Maybe because I have seen too much objectivity in my own school experiences is why I am reluctant to impose that upon others.

1982

The night for the Faulkner class had finally arrived. We met in the usual seminar room, even though the course was in an eight-by-ten room containing one blackboard stand and two tables, end to end, accommodating about fifteen students. I expected at least that amount or more since the class was both a 400-level (undergraduate) and a 700-level course (graduate) and since I expected others to share my genuine fondness for Faulkner literature by enrolling in the class. That evening, however, there were only eight to ten students in attendance and only one other graduate assistant besides myself, who, unlike the other nine assistants, took six hours of study instead of the ten hours of study. The syllabus explained how we would read eight novels, fifteen short stories, and do a fifteen to twenty-minute-oral report on the ninth novel of our choosing. There was to be one five-page-written paper required for graduates, also one ten-page-researched paper required for the graduate assistants. Each week, or each two weeks as it occasionally balanced out, as we began a new novel, we were to read two scholarly articles about that novel specifically listed in the *American Literary Scholarship* series from 1963 to 1973 and to write one typewritten page critiquing each article by testing the article against our own reading of the novel. The next week, we had five students enrolled in class, and one of the five was a teacher monitoring the course for five to six weeks. Out of the four enrolled students, one boy was a student on a government loan who had to qualify for being enrolled in a minimum amount of hours. By the end of the last week of the semester, three students had finished the course, one failed the course, one had a "C," and the other one had a "B," but then I am getting ahead of my story.

By the time of dismissal of our class at about 9:30 p.m., I was not that eager to begin reading a new novel. I enjoyed just walking around the various lighted pathways and blending into the intellectual night. The quietness and darkness of the campus, along with the campus chimes and reflecting lamps, offered a silent companionship that did not always exist in the daylight traffic of students who were regimented to a full-time schedule. The night was single and simple and seemed not to foreshadow any need to worry. Thus I felt like Scarlet O'Hara in *Gone With The Wind*. Rather than worry about all of my Faulkner assignments, I agreed with Scarlet: "I will think about it tomorrow."

The other classes required for my semester's schedule did not pose a problem nor demand an unusual or unreasonable amount of study. I quickly sized up my other three professors. In the Modern British Literature class, I knew from previous years that Dr. Hugh Kinney was tough, exact, erudite, extremely conservative, and a Harvard graduate. From previous years of taking courses at that college, I knew his lecture delivery to be dry, monotone, and in a "chairman-of-the-board" demeanor that established emphatically that one nodded in agreement when he nodded and laughed when (and if) he would laugh. Any deviation in the creative or the unique mode would jeopardize a decent grade from him for the whole semester. I accepted the code, and if evaluations were asked, I gave the correct response and gave "strongly agree" on every questionnaire — that was the expected code, and, thus, I accepted the implied behavioral expectation.

My other professor, Dr. Jared Whitney, I likewise knew from undergraduate study. He was the one choice I had for some deviation from the norm. He seemed to tolerate a certain amount of creativity, but I also recalled that it was through his teaching that I remembered my first disillusioning college experience. He had taught British Literature back in 1970, the year I transferred from Wakenda Community College to Southeast Kansas College. I thought studying British and American Literature was like rediscovering long lost relatives who shared the same heritage for the love of literature as I. At that time, I exalted in studying all of his assignments, never once relying on Cliff Notes as a "short cut" to reading. I did not want to be deprived of one abbreviated paragraph, and I reveled in memorization of lines of poetry for specific detail on tests. The sum total, however, of my study of British Literature for two semesters resulted in grades never over a "B" except for my creative papers. They merited an "A" with comments like "A most unique paper" or another comment, "A very original, interesting paper." Once Dr. Whitney announced to the class that my paper and another girl's paper were the two best papers in class. Still, when it came time for test feedbacks, I started out with a "D" on the first test and worked up no higher than a "B" the whole year. Finally, I decided to go to his office and ask him why I could not merit higher than a "B" out of the course. His answer was that maybe I was working too hard. That was the first time in all of my school years I have ever heard a teacher attempt to tell a student he or she was working too hard! One spends a lifetime as a teacher trying to motivate students to work hard in her class, and in a matter of five seconds, I had a teacher defy all concepts of motivation. When I left his office, I remember writing in my notebook:

> Will I never find
> Thy perfect flower
> To bear thy fruit
> And bloom each hour,
> To bring to life
> A sweet repose,
> To outgrow all the
> Weeds of woe.

Despite the disappointing experience from his course during my first "go-round" at college, I still preferred his gifted lectoral ability and humorous witticisms compared to the other less dynamic teachers, so I signed up for a second round of his teaching in my graduate study. In a period of ten years, between the time of my undergraduate study and my graduate work, the god-like man, who enthralled audiences with his charismatic personality, had aged noticeably the last twenty years, and I understood it was not because he had worked too hard on his courses. Since I last knew the tall, dark Dr. Whitney, he had divorced his wife, married one of his students, and divorced her five years later, remarried her, then divorced again another year later. He was now a nervous, less confident teacher obviously in need of either a cigarette in one hand or a cup of coffee in the other hand. Once we students noted that he held a book, a cup of coffee and a cigarette while delivering a lecture. His hair was now scraggly thin and typified most contemporary middle-age "available" men in that he was lean and "mod." The legendary Dr. Jared Whitney, who was known to knock on the doors of his female students late at night asking for a glass of beer (while discussing the classics), appeared before me now uncharacteristically unheroic as a matador having lost more fights than he ever won. In fact, it would be safe to say that Dr. Whitney possibly had been gored one time too many. Yet, there remained that compelling, romantic voice of his which, frankly, I found so attractive. I watched his current style of delivery, and suddenly it occurred to me: Does the man have a drinking problem? I told myself that this could be a most interesting semester — most interesting indeed!!

My last required course for the semester was by our supervisor. Her task was to meet with us once a week and provide our curriculum guidelines for the current week. These sessions also introduced us to various professional theories in education as well as gave us an outlet for discussing any problems that may have arisen within our classes. Jan Burns was a young, twenty-seven-year-old supervisor working on her doctorate degree. Certainly she was well versed in theory and was competent in methods. Whether she could maintain an application of practicality and common sense remained to be seen. At least on a surface level, she appeared to me that she could laugh and could be capable of humanistic teaching. My initial judgment was that the two of us were of opposite camps of philosophy when it came to teaching by the book, but perhaps in a one-on-one situation, we could communicate. After all, teachers of 101 communications courses should be able to communicate opinions and ideas.

• • • • • • • •
1953
• • • • • • • •

I wonder if most students can vividly recall the exact moment when they realized that, like Holden Caulfield in *The Catcher in the Rye*, there would not always be someone to "catch a body as he walks through the rye." My fall from innocence and naivete occurred in my senior year of 1953. Why a fall from innocence should take as long as one's senior year was indicative of the fifties. We were, after all, the "silent generation," the "inhibited generation," and exposure to the sophisticated world simply did not apply for most Midwest filial offsprings, especially for women, until she either went to work, college, or until she married. Only a small percentage of girls went to college. For those who chose work, and it was exactly that: WORK — not a "career" for women, so the most normal choice for girls was marriage. Symptomatic to all generations, however, is the need to dream and to aim for high ideals, whether they be entirely realistic or practical. At a stage when seniors began selecting an occupational choice for when they graduated, I visualized myself, at age eighteen, as a missionary in some remote, uncivilized part of the world, or if not that, then I considered choosing to be a doctor in order to perform noble, miraculous healing deeds for mankind. Sure, all of the "right stuff" for the heroic minded, I grant you, and when we finished our senior testing for vocation, intelligence, etc., I approached the guidance counselor to announce my noble intentions. The interview took only two minutes of "guidance" for the counselor to untactfully announce to me that I did not have the "right stuff" to become a missionary or a doctor. I said, "Well, why do I make all "A's?" He said, "Because you are well liked." I thought to myself, what is intelligence if it is not to be able to assimilate and to adapt to all people and to all circumstances? Wasn't there any way to measure that factor in their intelligence tests?

Constantly, I am amazed how guidance counselors (some, not all, and mostly endemic of pre-'60s) can amass hours and hours of psychology and still can so consistently be among the most tactless, uncommunicative people in education! I hate to come down hard on the psychology people, but the truth is I have seen a large percentage of psychology majors who could not look a person in the eye or relate to the most mundane concepts of everyday thinking, let alone be capable of identifying with the masses of humanity. A large percentage of psychology majors would seem to suffer from so many psychological hang-ups of their own, that it is almost beyond comprehension to see them struggle with other people's problems. I suppose the essence of the whole problem is that I basically do not believe "guidance" comes under the realm of tampering with dreams. The bottom line is that I believe the individual student in question is the best qualified person to know whether he or she can manage to be successful for a specific quest. I often heard the argument that if a teacher or coach or guidance counselor destroyed dreams for a student, then that dream or goal was not very strong in the first place. But I do not know about that. I think that in a situation where the student is economically limited, is socially restricted, and is lacking assertiveness, and is missing outside, adult influence, then in stifling, negative environments, the student can suffer irreparable harm. Coaches utilize every aspect of positive influence, but someone practicing the opposite techniques of encouragement conversely produces measurable, destructive results.

Before I get off of the subject of psychology, let me pass on several real-life experiences with the psychology department. Last year a friend of mine, Dan Hobson, asked me to pick up his psychology tests at Southeast Kansas College. He was taking one night course while teaching in the middle school at Wakenda. In fact, his class was on the same night as my Faulkner class, but where he drove back and forth to class from Wakenda, I lived in Caughburg, the home of Southeast Kansas College which was thirty miles south from Wakenda. When I asked Dan's professor to please release his papers and tests to me, the professor said, "Are you Dan's mother?" Now, really, how calculatingly unaware can a Ph.D. in psychology be in regard to the most rudiment of social etiquette? I mean everyone and anyone knows that one does not insult a woman by talking about her age!! The only decent answer to a question such as that would be to say: "No, he is just my lover — I get my kicks from younger boys." Or I could also answer, "Oh, yes, Dan is my illegitimate son — funny you should ask." But to a dreamer like myself, psychology is not taken that seriously.

• • • • • • • •
1953
• • • • • • • •

I proceeded through my senior year of high school with undaunted ambitions. My next scheme in 1953 was to look into the possibilities of following my athletic girlfriend, who was a year older than I and a grade ahead of me, to a private girls' school in Missouri in order that we could continue playing tennis together since there were no girls' teams in our local schools in the '50s. Tennis was the only sport offered to girls in other schools during the early '50s as a competitive team sport, and we considered ourselves talented (naturally) — at least good enough to make a team somewhere. In our location, and at that time of tennis history, if a girl happened to be good enough to play with the fellows, she was considered somewhat outstanding. Few girl athletes were capable of keeping up with the boys fast brand of tough tennis. One seldom found over a half-dozen girl tennis players in each town compared to three and four times that amount now.

I decided, therefore, to ask the principal about the chances of going on to college on an academic scholarship since I knew that my parents could not manage the expenses of a college education. At that time, only about one-tenth of the students' parents could afford to send their children off to college. Another characteristic of the time period was that we were certainly not gifted with so-called "humanistic" educators during the '50s. The typical "old maids" prevailed (though some excellently trained and prepared), but a student rarely said what he or she wanted to which, of course, was very stifling to say the least. Anyway on with the incident at hand. Sitting in the office facing one another, the principal informed me that I would not be happy going to a girls' private school. Much like the conversation with the guidance counselor, I was audacious enough (or prone to rebellion) to ask, "Why would I not be happy going there?" The principal said, "Most of the girls were well-to-do in that college, and he did not think I would be satisfied at that particular college." In other words, I was from the wrong side of the tracks; and you know that was the first time I had ever realized that I was. I just supposed that when I had as wonderful and happy childhood as I had had and as loving parents that I was blessed with having, then I could not possibly be from the WRONG side of the town. I thanked him for his advice and walked out.

Two years before my high school graduation in 1953, the same principal had called my sister into his office before she was to graduate in 1951 and told her that she had merited the valedictorian award based on the highest grade-point average throughout her fours years of high school, but because the boy who was one point behind her needed that award to assure him of a naval academy appointment, the principal had decided to switch the award to the young man instead of my sister. There was no debate, no discussion, no opposition, for indeed it was the "silent generation." Disappointments and disapprovals were quailed, but they were never forgotten, and that excoriated thinking was perhaps more harmful than the volatile expressions of the sixties and seventies.

The rest of my senior year I concentrated on making good grades and carrying out my duties of being elected the Senior Class President. Grades were never the means to an end for me; for example, I can remember always making dumb decisions based on idealism and principles rather than popularity. The Senior English teacher stopped at my desk one day to deliver grade cards, and she remarked that my "B" could be an "A" if I would orally recite. Somehow I had taken it upon myself to more or less boycott her demands because of her prejudice to students who were not in the "in-crowd," who were farm kids, and who were the black minority students, and although I felt I belonged to the in-crowd, I felt sorry for those who did not meet her "social" standards. I took the "B" for the senior year of English and moved my status of academic achievement to fourth place. I guess I interpreted being Senior Class President to having a responsibility and a commitment to everyone, and besides, I thought she was hypocritical to be nice only to her standards of the "chosen."

Most students in 1953 felt free to come to me with ideas and suggestions for our class which eventually led to my final fall. When students wanted to get the class motivated as a single, cooperative class unit, I came up with the original idea of voting for a king and queen by voting with pennies. At the end of the contest, we would turn the money over to the Lions Club which was in charge of the March of Dimes, and they, in turn, would honor our king and queen at their banquet, thereby accomplishing the threefold purpose of: (1) working as a class unit; (2) contributing to a worthy, charitable cause; and (3) bringing recognition to the king and queen honorees. The next thing I knew was that I was asked to come to the principal's office to answer the charge by the senior sponsor as to why I was trying to "run the school." What could I say? In their eyes, I was guilty, and, yes, I was guilty of creativity, initiative and "ole Yankee ingenuity." Five years later, the contest would become an annual event, and three years later, the same principal would be hung in effigy on the front lawn of the high school campus. But for the moment, for a seventeen-year-old idealistic young woman, tears were the only defense in the presence of such authority; it mattered little whether I was guilty of not. From the moment I left the office in tears to the time I returned to the safeness and sanctity of my home, I had been initiated and baptized into a philosophy of education that I would never forget. I vowed that if I became a teacher, I would at least know what NOT to do to an individual's pride and dignity. After high school, I went one semester to junior college, and then I quit school to get married the following spring. I did not plan to return to education.

••••••••
1982
••••••••

I looked at my 8:30 a.m. freshman composition class. They were punctual, disciplined, obedient and respectful. If I did not shake them out of that choreographic complacency, though, I would not have a successful class. Some times the material we study can provoke and stimulate discussion and controversy, but in freshmen composition at Southeast Kansas College, we were mainly confined to teaching out of one extremely poor grammar book and one text of sample short stories illustrating the techniques of various types of rhetorical styles and methods. The idea was that by reading a professional short story, the novice would be able to duplicate a similar style. And it ain't so! First, the teacher must reach the student's soul (or be it his heart or mind, depending upon one's religion) and tap his potentiality for expression. Teachers do that by either directly relating to contemporary ideas the students can relate to or by indirectly reaching a student through literature which mirrors the conditions of human existence, or preferably do both. But teachers must encourage the student to express himself and to be satisfied with what he disclosed about himself. The paper must be like a mirror reflecting the innermost personality of that particular student. After he can do that, he can study the masters. But none of us teachers in freshmen 101 composition were assigned novels to teach or films to watch other than special films pertaining to our subject matter, and those we did have available had to be requisitioned for viewing time outside of the regular English hour.

With ennui quickly settling in for the semester, I badly needed to provoke argument to unsettle my class' stagnation, and to do that often required playing the devil's advocate by inciting an argument. For example, one day we briefly talked about racial and political freedom. I decided to add fuel to the fire by asking whether animals should be chained? And should there be a leash law? If so, why? If not, why? When there did not follow immediate debate, I went into my "act" and tirade about the abuse of penned dogs and how it makes them mean and barking dogs and vicious, adding the tear-jerking examples of dogs chained to a six-by-six space sitting in their own excrements like prisoners of war. Finally, they were incited to retaliate with the usual humane responses of how it protects all of the little children not to have a "mad dog" on the loose. To conclude the success of the class involvement, I went to class the next day chained to a fellow teacher who led me to class and tied me to the desk!! At least I had stirred the thinking pot for a change instead of their smoking the pot and inanimately sitting muted all hour. The more I thought about the discussion afterwards, I decided English teachers' approach to English is quite similar to one's attitude toward the animal kingdom in general. In one camp there are those teachers who would chain student outlets of expression and try to harness the individual to a confined territory. In another camp there are those teachers who see the necessity of freedom of movement as being compatible with the freedom of spirit. Of course, there are the other teachers, too, who care very little for animals in the first place.

In our Faulkner class, we were well into our fourth week of the fall semester. I had handed in four critiques the first two weeks. The third week we did not meet, and so it was the fourth week before the Head of the Department returned all of the critiques. Every one of mine had the written instruction on it to "please redo," and yet I was ready to attempt the next two critiques in addition to preparing for my five-page researched paper and the oral report, all due within another three to four weeks. To say that I was extremely deflated at this point in my illustrious career was an understatement beyond belief. Not helping the situation was a lousy attitude on my part of considering the reports a superficial exercise in mimicry of scholarly reviews emanating dry, dull, and always with the right amount of affectation which contributed to scholarly "suck up."

I asked the foreign student, Mary Ann Sayaad, if she knew whether revisions were the usual procedure for the course. Mary Ann told me: "I have known or heard of students having to rewrite the reports not only once, but also three or four times. Very few of us foreign students take that course and pass." My decision was made: I would forge ahead and do all of the assignments on their scheduled due date, and any and all other rewrites would simply have to wait for revisions until the Christmas vacation. Anyway, I knew for a fact that the Head of the Department's girlfriend, Connie, was completing work on her Faulkner class she had had two semesters prior to our class!! Therefore, I took it for granted that that must be the accepted process for graduate assistants when subjected to above and beyond the call of duty assignments. That was a grave, erroneous assumption on my part. I thus proceeded ahead with my Faulkner reading list with about as much as enthusiasm as a draft dodger entering Fort Leavenworth — the results having the same impending disaster.

Meanwhile, we were well into our freshmen composition instruction by my supervisor, Jan Burns, and I already was losing patience with the whole freshmen composition system being revolved around a nonsensical method of grading. I was beginning to believe that Ms. Burns' lack of classroom experience, despite the fact that she had a doctor's degree at age twenty-seven, was producing well-intended methods of grading, but unsound. The student textbook on grammar was being highly criticized on all fronts by the students as well as the teachers. Personally, I did not aggressively object, for it mattered little to me since I had dismissed the book as useless about the second week of the semester. What grammar I included in my class, I used from my own material and my own resources. The supervisor mentioned to me in one of our weekly one-on-one conferences that I was causing myself a considerable amount of extra grading by writing constructive criticisms on each paper and naming the error that the student had made. She suggested that I use the department's system of grading whereby we graduate assistants give each error on students' papers a code lettering for the rule violation explained in the book of the grammar text. If, for instance, a violation of pronoun and antecedent agreement occurred on a student's paper, the teacher would assign the code violation like "6q;" run-on sentences would be "14b;" unnecessary change in tense "8f;" etc. What it all boiled down to was that the student was subjected to a three-step process of memorization on rules of grammar: First, he must memorize what the numbers signify; second, he must memorize what the letters signify with each numbering system; and last, he must memorize the rule governing that infraction. In addition to this repetitive redundancy, the department had a phobia on commas, and papers could be flunked for not demonstrating a knowledge on how to use commas. The department had a neat, gift-wrapped-packaged deal out of the six rules for commas. Instead of using a comma for introductory phrases and clauses, we were to call them introductory elements. In the place of non-restrictive noun and adjective clauses, they were named interrupters. Anything set off by a comma from the core sentence was called an "afterthought" thereby creating all types of fragmented core sentences. Has anyone ever tried writing sentences containing afterthoughts, or for that matter, is anything worth writing considered an afterthought? The rules game had all of the makings of excellent material for one of George Carlin's routines on language.

Of course, what all of us graduate assistants encountered under the new comma system was the embarrassing dilemma of explaining what was the purpose of clauses and phrases. How can a student recognize he has a fragment without first understanding the function and usage of clauses and phrases, or how can one achieve good parallelism without a good understanding and recognition of clauses and phrases? In addition, I felt that I could not teach student paragraph coherence, sentence variety and transitional devises without first having a basic review on phrases, clauses and transitions. How can a teacher possibly grade a paper on commas if students do not understand restrictive and non-restrictive clauses and phrases. By the middle of the semester, most of the other freshmen classes were still writing paragraphs, but my class had written three, five-paragraph themes, and I was faithful to the conviction that practice made perfect. Besides, I liked to make the students constantly formulate new ideas and subjects worthy of writing assignments.

On the three papers I had graded for my students, my advisor reviewed my grading comments and complimented my grading techniques by saying I gave the most positive, helpful comments to my students than any of the other graduate assistants. I appreciated the compliment, thanked her and explained that my methods were sometimes unorthodox, but in all sincerity I explained that I had been fortunate in studying from a great English teacher in the community college in my hometown of Wakenda who had been consistently judged not by educators alone as an outstanding teacher, but also she had consistently, almost one-hundred percent, been accepted and acclaimed by every student taking her program. Those same students went on to attest to her unique ability as a teacher when they compared her methods to other teachers in other universities. The education department at Southeast Kansas College once told me that 99 percent of the students enrolling at their college asked for this dynamic woman as one of their letters of recommendations. Who better to judge us as merit teachers than the students? Yet, we teachers often react with fear and scorn at the possibility of students taking that responsibility. But students KNOW, and they are very wordly-wise — I never like to underestimate them.

ON THE SUBJECT OF GRADING: The department's policy for grading at Southeast Kansas College, and for passing the freshman 101 English course, was either pass or fail. There was certainly no in between, and the whole idea could not have been more frustratingly funny, as well as sad, to teach with a dictum of "either/or." Naturally, a teacher was to begin a course with returning a quantity of "F" papers, all under the guise of motivation, of course. I could never, out of a sense of duty, feel that for one minute I could "con" a student. If the student felt that he wrote with the "gut" or with the heart, and he managed to deliver, then the least I could do as a teacher was to give positive encouragement and always positive criticisms. Ineffective and inexperienced teachers usually delight and revel in catching a student in an error or to make them look like fledging freshmen floundering at the learned professor's feet. Go into a faculty lounge, and one can record one-half of the conversation centered around wrongs, not rights. Also, I was "vulnerable" on this issue of student-fault-finding since I was simultaneously subjected to so many "redos" in my Faulkner class. Likewise on the freshman 101 papers we graded, every error (regardless of how minute) was to be recorded in their individual student files, to be corrected, and to be rewritten until a passing grade could be given. I subscribed to the theory that three different five-paragraph themes which tax the thought processes were far more valuable that rehashing yesterday's news. Each to his own.

An example of diversified opinion and conflict about grading was to attend a practice grading session for all of the graduate assistants and several of the tenured faculty members teaching 101 English. In the two grading sessions I attended, not one of the four to five-member groups, out of the four groups of about sixteen to twenty teachers, held a consensus of opinion as to what constituted an "A" or "F" paper. In one session, the dialogue went something like this. The tenured faculty professor spoke up and said that a paper should say something interesting, at least. The advisor replied, "Are you saying that ideas are more important than fundamentals?" and he answered, "Well, hell, yes. Ultimately the damn paper should have something to say and not be boring." That was dear Dr. Whitney speaking.

In our weekly graduate assistant seminar oral reports, there was increasingly voiced concern over having to give so many "F" grades. But on the other side of the spectrum, the boss's girlfriend exclaimed how she was sick and tired of students not writing anything but "F" papers nor not having any participation in class discussions (as if she were forced to give upteen-hundred "F's). She said, "I finally reversed roles with them and made all of them go to the front of the room and orally explain their papers while I sat as the audience and became the bored, complaining audience that they portrayed everyday to her. In almost the same breath, I heard her ask an in-service visiting educator to our seminar class what a teacher could do when students act belligerent toward her. If one has to ask, need any more be said! Tragically, though, with her intelligence, ambition, and apparent "higher connections" she would typify the scholars in pursuit of the doctorate degrees who would one day return to teach teachers how to teach, or some such similar position commensurate with her degree. Finances and time should not be equated with requirements necessary for the doctorate diploma. When I attended Southeast Kansas College ten years ago, in 1970, the Head of the English Department at that time told me that a doctor's degree was the undoing of a teacher! This theory should be explored in its fullest ramifications for the recruiting of the best and the brightest of educators.

My turn had arrived for an oral offering of my class's progress report. The whole morbid, negative, "henny-penny- progress reports on our freshmen classes struck me as funny, and so I began simulating a very frank teacher-student talk for my graduate assistants' audience with my *imaginary* student:

> "Oh, hello, there, Abe. Yes, come on in. First of all, Able, you are late, and now that you are in college, you need to discipline your priorities. Oh, I know you said that you had to walk twenty miles to school, but come on now, you can't believe the excuses we get as teachers. Why, for instance, one time a student said that his father kept him home because he had chopped down a cherry tree! Another student told me that he had been up all night riding horseback through every middle sex, village and farm, and he was too tired to get to school. So come on, Abe, try to be a little more responsible. After all, we have standards in this department.
>
> "Now about this composition. What's that you ask? Do you have to rewrite it? No, not exactly — just make a few corrections and suggestions that I have written on the back of the composition — below the "F." For example, you begin the paper with "Four score and seven years ago our forefathers ....' Abe, think of your audience. You are writing for teachers, not students, and many of them do not know what the score is, so try to open with a more simple, direct approach like ... like ... 'once upon a time ....' Yes, I like that. Make the change.
>
> "Now, down here you say 'Testing whether that nation or any other nation.' Which do you mean, Abe? Any nation can, of course, mean any nation in the

whole damn universe, so please be more specific. Also, you tend to digress to generalities such as, 'they gave the last full measure of devotion.' Abe, can you really measure devotion? I have circled that error as a 14b — look it up. And again, here is another example of ambiguity and generality, Abe, because you say, 'the world will little remember.' Little remember is like little do or little say, Abe. Just don't put down the first adjective that comes to your freshman mind. Now here you say, 'of the people, by the people and for the people.' That is so sing-songy, Abe. In a good, solid, fundamental essay, we structure with clarity and correctness like 'the people and all of those hereto.' Yes, that sounds better as well as corrects your tendency to write in simple, four-syllable choices of words. You walk back home, Abe, and see if you can't have the revisions by 8:30 a.m. Okay? Yes, goodday, Abe, and thanks for dropping by ... Bye-bye." (Sigh). I sometimes wonder if that boy will ever amount to anything!!

After that parody on our grading system, I settled down to seriousness and to concentrate on my first lengthy paper for my Faulkner class. I was doing a critical analysis over *Light In August*. I had chosen the theme "The Determined Determinism in *Light In August*." As the title immediately indicated, I was not totally convinced of the impetus my theme would convey. However, the Head of the Department had suggested, with his usual pomposity, that we first get his OK on a selected topic, so when he suggested determinism for my paper, I decided that it would be more beneficial to have him happy rather than to delight myself with another ego-trip writing experiment which I normally liked to do. I literally groped through the major part of the theme without a great deal of purpose and direction, I will admit. When I came to my conclusion, I could tolerate it no longer, and so I yielded to the instinctive impulse of writing that, for me, frequently alleviated the obvious and obdurate necessities of critical analysis. I decided to put a "requiem scene" dialogue for my conclusion. My reasoning for the creative decision was that in my amateur analysis, the book conveyed two major themes: One theme was the tragic portrayal of people who, through either fatalism or determinism, never managed to escape the "darkness" of living. In other words, they never scored, they never won, and they never flowed with the human tide of fulfillment or success. The second major theme in *Light In August* was the depiction of an inactive, decadent religion capable of very negative destruction when used in the context of narrow-minded, hypocritical characters. Often in Faulkner's novels, border-line schizophrenic, zealot individuals apply the scriptures and religious doctrine without an awareness of the present social obligation for involvement in the human aspects of religious needs and compassions. They are often fanatics attempting an eye-for-an-eye religion or either passive followers using the theme that "the meek shall inherit the earth" as justification for turning the other cheek rather than righting the injustices of society.

By the end of the paper, I had sensed a "feel" for the style and mood of Faulkner in *Light In August*, so I reasoned that that discovery alone was probably the most important purpose for the study of Faulkner. What more could a novelist want than to know his readers understood his expressions of a universal conflict of man? How better to express my appreciation of the thematic content of *Light In August* than to duplicate in tone, style and theme the essence of Faulkner philosophy. Naturally, I was making all of the wrong, subjective assumptions forbidden in a formal critical analysis paper, but the dye was cast, and I was too caught up in the enthusiasm of writing to entertain the idea that the Head of the Department would not see what I was attempting to project. Hence, I wrote my version of a requiem scene for the end of *Light In August*.

By the eighth week of the term, I eagerly went to my Faulkner class hoping that our papers would be returned and hoping the last page of my paper would contain a comment similar to the Head of the Department's comments on my papers in 1970 such as: "A very different paper, but it does get to the heart of the matter. 'A.' " Well, I opened my *latest* paper and read the *latest* boss's remarks: "The purpose of this assignment is to give you guidance in writing a scholarly research paper as a novel by William Faulkner. Your paper is not suitable in either tone, matter or method to this purpose. Please do the paper over."

By the time I left class that evening, I hardly remembered whether it was night or day or what the campus chimes were playing. All noises seemed muted in comparison to what was shouting at me in my subconscious. PLEASE REDO. REDO. REDO. REDO ....

I hurried home and immediately called my friend Stan Warren in Kansas City. Stan and I shared three years of teaching together in high school in Wakenda from 1973 to 1976. He had left the teaching field because of adversity, too, and had entered medical school in 1982. We had remained friends through the years and through the adversity, and recently he had especially been a confidant and advisor in my recent divorce proceedings. Finally, I reached him about eleven o'clock in the evening, and by that time I was in uncontrollable sobs. He said later that he could not remember hearing me in such a state of desperation, even through my divorce. I said that I had received the straw that breaks the camel's back. I was not sure whether I could continue with trying to regain a career. The culmination of coping with a new home, new career and altogether new lifestyle was multitudinous in problems. Up to that point, I had usually been able to see a funny side of a problem along with the sad aspect of it all. For example, after the divorce, I bought a tool box as a show of total independence, both mentally and physically, but the first thing that broke in my household was the tool box lid, and I could not fix it! Or there was the time when my husband had moved out, and after about one month, when he came back for additional supplies such as sheets, I said, "Will that be one pillowcase or two?" Now, though, I brooded that I had momentarily been defeated in every sense of the word, but I also knew that I had 100 percent backing by all of my family and friends, and I also kept in mind that many of those supporters had gone way beyond the call of duty in helping me to regain a semblance of roots and permanence once again. They had given help and love as I had never experienced nor witnessed at any time in my life, and I loved them for that "test" which subjected all of our beliefs and values — I owed them a great deal.

Stan said to hang on until the weekend when we would discuss a "counterattack." He reminded me that I had come too far to be discouraged by an S.O.B. professor!! I cried through the night, met my 8:30 a.m. college class I taught the next day, and then I "skipped" the rest of the day. I walked my half-blind, half-deaf dog the next day and talked to her about a "dog's life." I wondered if she ever wished to be put to sleep in preference to the combat of survival of the elements. The coldness of the winter was setting in, and I would particularly have to watch whether she would be capable of enduring another cold winter. If she cried out as if in pain, or began bleeding, I knew I would have to put her to sleep. For now, I needed her badly to help see me through the harshness of the nature of the season and the nature of man's inhumanity to man. We would stick together and somehow just try to make it through the week; then we would decide on a future course of action.

• • • • • • • •
1969
• • • • • • • •

About fifteen years after my high school graduation, I decided to continue my education at a local community college. My children were ages nine, twelve and thirteen and were beginning to need me less and less as a full-time mother. This was at a particular education era (late '60s and early '70s) when adult education and continuing adult education were considered the American way of life. Education had reached a prominence of buy and sell students through all types of government loans, and suddenly education was big business, and minds and bodies could be traded on the market as easily as corn, oats and barley on a bullish trade season. Eagerly, the colleges and universities and community colleges began vying for student head counts, and, thus quickly institutions relaxed academic standards in order to accommodate the masses and not just the academians. Within a very short time in the early '70s, the educational systems were advertising metaphorically, "give me your tired, your poor, your huddled masses," and I will find a way to reward them with a degree of some sort. Hence, the push for degree certification metamorphosed into a conglomerate of open-door competition within the educational system, and the rewards for doing business within the ivy walls were the guarantees that most students would move down the assembly line of classes with a diploma waiting for them at the end of four years, just in time to qualify for the promises of money and success in the job market. For potential draft dodgers, a college education with above-average grades would forestall the inevitable Vietnam draft selection possibly three or more additional years. Colleges and universities experienced "boom" years never surpassed since post World War II when the government's military policies encouraged college enrollments with the G.I. Bill. Cynically, one could almost deduce that war is one viable pathway to knowledge.

 In retrospect, I believe that I reentered education (after a fifteen-year-old hiatus) through monetary rewards in the form of educational loans. At the time, my husband was coaching and recruiting, and he literally campaigned for my returning to school. He handled the applications for loans and managed the banking of those loans while all I had to do was to attend school. Well, that wasn't all I had to do. We had just bought our first home: a rambling, two-story, eleven-room house, and we were well into the initial stages of plastering and trying to build a kitchen out of a very old kitchen. Besides that, I was teaching three daily classes in tennis for boys and girls ages eight to eighteen. No, I can't remember thinking that I needed something to occupy my time. Nevertheless, my husband felt the time was financially right to return to school, and I deferred to his wise judgment since he was an educator also. Looking back, I wish the desire for learning had been for the purest of reasons, but I am not convinced I was encouraged to return to school for ALL of the *right* reasons. I would really like to believe I did; yet, where money is THE determining factor, there frequently exists a tainted truth underneath one's history of "ulterior motives."

To add to the uncertainty of whether I belonged back in school, I was basically very shy in unfamiliar territory. I looked at all of the young students shuffling actively through the halls, and I felt much older than my thirty-five years. If I could have slipped into class relatively unnoticed and managed to sneak to the back of the room, I knew I could probably survive the first day at college. I was elated to find that there were three or four other "older" students in the American Literature class, so we non-traditionalists gravitated to one another as a means of both offense and defense to an overwhelming majority of youth going to school. In all due respects to college students, however, I have found, through the years, that fear of age differences between students in college is entirely unfounded and unwarranted because youth create no barriers in age prejudices. Never was I treated but with the warmest and kindest of cordiality. Maybe we were all companions and cohorts of an age thrust into several decades of dissent and disillusionment with many of our American traditions. If there was any biasism on age within the universities at that time, the attitude manifested itself within the ranks of the traditionalist teachers, not students. At least that was true for the students ranging in the "older" group category. As proof, advice began filtering through channels of communication among the students that to beware of certain teachers who were known to vocally express the belief that older women belonged at home with their children and not in pursuit of a career. As unbelievable as that may seem to women of the twenty-first century, the late '60s and early '70s did not view women as completely liberated. Many, including professors, clung to traditional concepts about the roles of women and men in marriage, and actually, and ironically, at that time, I totally agreed with the popular belief that a woman's place was at home and that a man definitely wore the pants in the family. Evidence of my acceptance of this was, of course, the fact that I was convinced by my husband that I should finish my education. The climate in the colleges during the rebellious sixties and the angry seventies fermented such diversity and turmoil that I merely tried to blend in with the conservative elements and watch from a sideline the questioning and rebelling of this generation.

There was a time, during the interval of attending college from 1969 to 1972, when I could refrain no longer from committing myself to how I felt about the student college revolts. To remain passive or indifferent to the turbulent decade of the '70s was almost to admit silence denoted consent, and that was almost as un-American and treasonous to education as the revolts were to the cause of upheaval and disruption within classrooms. I did not like my right for peaceful assemblage to be denied when we students went to hear Strom Thurmond speak in the Southeast Kansas College student union, or rather he tried to speak, but he was denied that right when hooded demonstrators sat on the stage and ridiculed and harassed his every statement. Several days later, the same demonstrators burned debris on the campus lawn, and that, to me, impinged upon the sacredness of the very foundations of the hallowed grounds of our institutions. Intelligent action was to debate, not to debauch. And so I indignantly entered the revolt by committing myself to law and order by voicing my opinions to the college newspaper. Ironically, in 1970, I used a quote from William Faulkner as I wrote:

"William Faulkner once said to University of Virginia students, 'It (education) should be a privilege, people should be willing to walk for or five miles to get to school.' Believe it or not, there are many of us in America, and, yes, even in Southeast Kansas College who believe education is a most prized possession. But unfortunately, surveys are never taken on how many students are in college to inculcate their ability and knowledge for future application.

"Despite the fact that there are students participating in acts of disobedience, violence, law-breaking infractions and unpeaceable assemblage where bricks, stones and vandalism normally accompany the right to peaceful assemblage, there are many others who are desirous of an education where politics does not dominate nor dictate to our educational systems.

"Since a number of our leading universities (prestige universities as the term originated) have chosen to lead us into the paths of unrighteousness, and apparently Dr. Samuels (college president) saw fit to include himself and Southeast Kansas College as among the "prestige," I purport separating those who would choose to use our educational institutions as playpens for false prophets from those who would walk five miles to school and who would scrape and dig for every nickel and dime in sight in order to have the privilege of paying for a college education.

"I also propose separating those who would suggest change, but offer no solutions from those who would suggest change by rolling up their shirt sleeves and working with our youth as coaches, teachers and guidance counselors, or who would go among the poor, the mentally retarded, the emotionally ill and the illiterate.

"I further suggest a separation of those teachers who would utilize paid classroom time for the purpose of propagating the policies of politics from the other teachers who are still disciples of a profession dedicated to the proposition that there is truth in teaching.

"If we be deluded and disillusioned into blindly following fools and cowards who would burn in the dark of the night, then I say close the doors of all of our universities and let the so-called leaders of tomorrow at least burn by the light of day so that all who care to witness might be enlightened by dissent.

"In *The Rubaiat of Omar Khayyam*, Edward Fitzgerald wrote, 'A hair perhaps divides the false and true.' Rather ironic that 111 years later, we truly have been divided and separated from truth and falsehood by a hair — a minority, to be sure, but a number of *long* hairs."

That was the extent of my involvement with college revolts, and the response was due, in part, to an incident during a particular night at Southeast Kansas College whereby students took over several offices, threw furniture out a window and burned it on the college grounds. One of my research papers in the community college had been about the book recently published called *The Berkeley Revolt* which piqued my interest because of the volatile times. My politics usually leaned "left," though where education was concerned, I retained a sense of idealism to the cause of knowledge.

• • • • • • • •
1969
• • • • • • • •

I walked into my first class since 1953 and looked up at my American Literature teacher (the same one I referred to earlier when I was mentioning her to my advisor). As she began her lecture, I knew immediately that this was the teacher — the great teacher — I had looked for all of my life. Her dramatic speaking voice emanated from a red-haired, five-foot-two, sixty-year-old petite frame. Her eyes pierced through to each student as if to tell each that she knew their mettle through and through. I knew I could never put anything over on that wise, discerning woman because she would spot fakery instantly. Inwardly, I believe I had always hoped there would be a teacher capable of imposing her will over mine. This woman I knew lacked not the temerity nor the initiative to shake the devil himself out of a student if he failed to respond to his fullest potential. Helen Keller had the fate and fortune to have a similar type of teacher. This teacher would personify the three qualities I believed necessary for a unique, great teacher and that was wisdom, intelligence and a sense of humor. Rarely are those three qualities endowed to one teacher.

I began two years of community college study in literature and English from that woman, and subsequently began for the first time in my life to be excited with education. I wanted to make up for twelve years of uneventful education in high school (with the exception of four or five enjoyable teachers) and explore authors and ideas in literature that I never realized existed. I literally soared with inspirational enthusiasm. I can only sum up those short, happy two years at a junior college by offering the poem I wrote which expressed the innate joy of the discovery of literature:

> You have warmed my soul with inspiration,
> You have kindled my mind with thoughts,
> Thoughts that smoldered without creation.
> You have ignited my quest for learning,
> You have inflamed my life with dreams,
> Dreams that were but ashes of yearning.
> And what have I to share with thee?
> Only my fire, ever burning.

Through various lectures, this great teacher told us about sharing ourselves, and she had taught us about the significance of each individual's contribution to society and the need for tolerance for the expression of beliefs, regardless of whether anyone disagreed or agreed. She taught us to respect the musician whether we like the music or not and to give appreciation to the athlete even if we did not participate in athletic events. She emphasized the point that artists are usually different from what we often mistakenly term "normal," but it is these artists who add beauty to our lives, so we should learn to remain open-minded to the new and different, cultural exposures to our lives.

Since she espoused a philosophy that I totally agreed with in ideology, I decided to show her the poem I attempted illustrating extended metaphor of conceit and discuss further the esthetics of literature. She agreed to meet me at a designated time and day in her office. Normally I would never have considered the bravado of meeting a teacher and sharing very private, personal feelings, but she had tapped resources in me that I had kept dormant and unexplored for so long that I could no longer lock them up inside and avoid sharing with others. The hour came, and she never arrived at her office or at the arranged hour. The hour came and went and was never to surface again. Like the poet Matthew Arnold wrote, "The choice goes by forever 'twixt that darkness and light.' "

Echoing and resounding for a lifetime will be priceless teaching tidbits she gave to hundreds and hundreds of students who sat at her feet in hero-worship adulation. I remember several of her priceless gems to us:
(1) "I am not much, but I am all you have."
(2) "A good teacher is a good actor."
(3) "I do not have to suffer fools."
(4) "I will sing for you or dance for you — whatever it takes to excite you to learn."
(5) "Be willing to walk to school if there is no available transportation. I have done this myself when the car broke down. It is important always to show up."
(6) For athletes arriving to the college from New Jersey, Chicago, etc., she would have guest speakers for assemblies and have the young ladies serve tea and cookies because she thought many should be "exposed to culture."
(7) "If you do not like the violin, at least pretend that you do as this will strengthen your character to present an interested, intelligent face."

1982

The weekend had arrived, and Stan and I hashed over the latest Faulkner class bad news. We contemplated my next move to redeem myself from what was quickly digressing into a losing proposition. His advice was very sound, for he suggested that I go see another professor, the second in command in the department, a good friend of Stan's and my academic advisor, and find out from him if I should continue the class or if I should withdraw before the final date for dropping a class was to expire the following week. Also, Stan reassured me that if I would finish the course (for after all the course was already three-fourths completed), then he would help me work on all rewrites during the Christmas vacation. Those were exactly the words I needed to hear because in every sense of the word I lacked confidence enough to rewrite a single paragraph, and the mere thought of trying to please the department Captain Bligh weakened me to a point of nausea. I kept my state of emergency to myself around the other graduate assistants, for I was too embarrassed to have the G.A.'s become aware of my demise within the department.

I did confess my problem to my advisor since she had to be warned that there were difficulties in my studies which could influence the effectiveness of my teaching responsibilities. When I confided in Jan, she said that all graduate students are confronted with overdue papers at one time or another, but she advised me to hand in whatever I could on the due dates, and she sympathetically added that very few graduate students have the time to submit quality work — it just went with the territory and a fact of life necessary for survival through graduate school. Also, we were well into our ninth week of the Faulkner course, and I, as yet, had no grade from the course on any of my work to indicate whether I was doing "F" work or somewhere above "F." Jan Burns pointed out to me that I should go and visit with the Head of the Department about our problem. She added that she had found him to be a really nice guy to talk with about solutions to departmental problems. (The following year she would resign her position.)

My next move was to follow up Stan's advice and go see the other teacher, Dr. Hugh Kinney, who was in charge of our Master's credentials and requirements and who was the second in command within the English Department. His unostentatious, low-key mannerisms had a way of making one feel relaxed and at ease once one was in his office. The almost complete graying of his hair added to his dignity of his duties, and many students sought his kind, astute counsel. Dr. Kinney asked me what was the problem in my Faulkner class. I began by explaining that my writing did not seem to please the boss and that everything I had written had been returned with the comment, "please redo." I explained to Dr. Kinney that I was no longer capable of rewriting through the night and being able to function as a teacher the next day. He agreed and even affirmed that that was true for him, too. Also, I said that I realized I had been out of school ten years, and I was a bit rusty with the technical phase of writing, but that I did expect to improve as the semester progressed. The question loomed as to whether I had the time and the stamina? I was pleased with the sagaciousness of Dr. Kinney's next statement. He said, "Go see the Head of the Department and if one of two things happened, if (1) he acted indifferent to my dropping the course or if (2) he encouraged me to drop, then I should probably go ahead and drop the class." There was still time to withdraw at the admissions office without having the class or grade on my transcript. I knew what I had to do.

If I had had the choice between a beating or a confrontation with the Head of the Department, I would have shouted for joy for the beating! Yet the task remained ahead. I was scared as I had never been before in facing an authority figure. I prayed I would not succumb to shaking, or having my voice quiver, or feeling the redness creep from my toes to my face, all of which I had humiliatingly experienced in times of formal, oral presentations or with intimidating, authoritative adults. No one experiencing his legs shaking and his voice quivering like a Don Knotts vibrato voice can ever empathize with that awful, panicky feeling.

The Head of the Department was at his desk when I entered, no doubt composing another one of his poems to be published in *The Midwest Quarterly*. As I sat down, he said quite business like, "What can I do for you, Amy?" I replied, "Well, apparently I did not merit a graduate assistantship based upon my writing ability." He acted almost surprised and added, "What did I mean?" I continued with saying that it seemed that everything I wrote was returned, and consequently this had placed me behind in the Faulkner course as well as affecting my work in other courses. I reiterated what I had told Dr. Kinney that I simply could not burn the midnight oil and be a positive force for my students the next day. Then I took a deep breath and added that I was considering dropping the course. His ensuing dialogue neither was discouraging nor apathetic, and he suggested, "It is too bad, Amy, that you do not write as well as you speak. In your writings, you tend to write metaphorically, but I want you to write with clarity and precision." I asked, "Is scholarship always compatible with good teaching because I am a teacher, not a scholar." He countered with dogmatically stating "that good writing was synonymous with good teaching, and it was perhaps the greatest gift we could give to a student who was entering our college." I said that I agreed, but it just seemed that in writing a report over a critical analysis, we were only parroting someone else's thoughts, and I considered that close to plagiarism. I believed our first obligation as educators was to encourage original thinking and to develop that thinking to its infinite potential.

He did not anger at this accusation, but repeated the need to analyze objectively a worthy piece of literature and to respond to that assignment in a concise, scholarly manner in direct proportion to the worthiness of the genius of William Faulkner. He further suggested: "I cannot decide for you as to whether you should drop the class or not — that is your decision, but I am one of the leading authorities on William Faulkner in the Midwest, and you have the opportunity to learn from a knowledgeable researcher about a difficult but brilliant novelist." I said that I would think it over during the weekend and let him know my decision. By the following Tuesday, I was back in the Faulkner class, determined to finish the course and to complete every assignment — at least the first time around on the writing assignments. After our talk, though, I never did receive back any of the one-page reports with any of the habitual comments such as "please redo." I detected an easing of pressure and hassle after our talk, but I still had one more paper to write (the ten-page paper), and seven more weeks remained in the course. I knew that I was not home safe by any sense of the word, nor was there any reason to think too optimistically on my grade at that point, either.

My other classes were typical: arduous and listless as they had been ten years ago! The one class which I had expected to be lively ("Men, Women and Love In Literature") by the one professor who had commanding magnetism (Dr. Whitney) had digressed to in-class-group reports about the current novel under study, plus hour-long-periodic, in-depth reports (sometimes two hours long) from all of the graduate students who were assigned individual reports on the philosophies of love by authors like Plato, Rollo May, Wylie Syphor, Migueldo Unamuno. Undergraduates in the class were responsible for short quizzes, one mid-term examination, a final exam and one ten-page paper. Graduate students were to accomplish the same except they were to give the oral hour-long individual report along with the class group report and to submit a somewhat longer term paper than undergraduates.

Our quizzes never materialized for the some forty or more students enrolled in our class, nor was a mid-term examination ever given which can help one know exactly what to expect by final time and where one is averaging in capability. After the course was three-fourths over, we students surmised that our final grade would be determined by the one paper, the final exam, and the oral report of us graduate students. In other words, there were no grades given until the day of the final when our report papers were returned to us. As for assessing our contributions to group reports and individual oral graduate presentations, we had no way of knowing whether our report was what Dr. Whitney expected or what he considered was "A" or "B" quality. In a situation such as that, we only tried to evaluate our own reports in accordance with audience reaction and response, or we tried to compare our reports to fellow peers. That usually resulted in inaccurate evaluations since one naturally sees oneself as either being on the same level with the "brains," or possibly even above their level of achievement. Unrealistic as that may seem, the inflated opinion of oneself is an honest human frailty sustained by perpetual democratic, grade-inflated education. We are democratically educated to believe that everyone is equal thereby merging equality with opportunity and creating classrooms to accommodate the "majority." But nowhere are the disparate differences so noticeable as when a class is introduced to oral presentations. Very few students can deliver an interesting oral report. One does not have to observe a class too often, nor be the most perceptive in observational powers to arrive at that conclusion. In fact most students read their oral reports, and, consequently, instant boredom sets in. In addition to lacking an audience awareness and an audience involvement, another characteristic of most oral reports is that few students do not know when to terminate a report, but instead, they invariably go over the allotted time — not five to ten minutes, but many extend a fifteen-minute report into a half-hour and hour-long reports. I have seen the record set by one graduate student who extended her report to "two days!" Why the teachers allow this to happen is more than I can phantom.

In the class "Men, Women and Love in Literature," the undergraduates outnumbered the graduate students, so many of the graduate students were becoming impatient with what they considered were "amateur" reports from the various groups in the class. Any number of vitriolic criticisms and satirical comments reverberated through the halls and individual graduate assistants' offices. The "Grandma" of the grad assistants had assumed leadership in what was amounting to serious intentions of vocally protesting the quantity of oral reports that we could endure in one college year. By the time I returned from teaching my 8:30 class one morning, I entered my office in the middle of a heated discussion with five or six of the graduate assistants.

Rebecca was speaking adamantly, "I have reached the limit of my tolerance in hearing those stupid oral reports. We could skip two weeks and never miss a thing. I am sick and tired of being bored to death with reports, and, personally, I think it is time we did something about it."

The cheerleader, Leslie, looked at this possibility of friction, and she said, "What do you mean, Rebecca? What could we do about it anyway?"

Rebecca looked at her almost condescendingly, as a parent to a mere child and said, "What could *we* do about it? *We* do not have to do anything, but I know what *I* am going to do, and if the rest of you will agree with me in principle, then I will go and speak to Dr. Whitney and say that on behalf of the graduate assistants enrolled in the class (which totaled six of us), we do not believe that it is fair to pay for a class to be taught by those knowing less than we do about the subject matter. I will remind him that we paid for his teaching knowledge, and we want him to teach, not the class do the teaching. After all, he is the one renowned for interesting, intellectual-lecture content. Will the rest of you back me on this?"

Two or three immediately agreed. The black graduate assistant, James Boyd, never decided any policy matters hurriedly or without deep, philosophical discussions, usually taking the discussion in so many different directions that eventually the group was in a quagmire of a debate. Ultimately, he held to the one main argument that he did not want to "rock the boat." By that he meant that the digression to lengthy oral reports in the class at least stalled for him the inevitable due paper and his own oral report, not to mention the necessity of reading all of the books he had yet to finish for the semester. I inwardly laughed, wondering if he was more behind than I knew myself to be. Perhaps my one Faulkner class predicament was the norm for about all of James's classes, and so the old saying, "it could be worse," won out again. About that time, Rebecca turned to me and asked how I voted? I said that I agree in principle, too, but disagree with her right to include all of us graduate assistants solidly behind the protest, for I could not support a vocal opposition to the professor's methods. I realized that I had piqued a sensitive subject because a silence permeated the office like the aftermath of a bad storm. Now I was obligated to attempt to explain myself or suffer the ostracizing of my fellow colleagues.

"Hey, gang, don't look at me as if I am the enemy — hear me out. It's just that I believe in the old axiom that if you have to tell someone how to be a good teacher, etc., he will not be a good teacher. Even if we were to correct a flaw in one area, a new flaw will emerge somewhere else. I've seen it happen. If you visit long enough in a faculty lounge, you will recognize that it would be very possible to suddenly announce to the faculty that you had discovered a secret, miraculous system of grading that was producing fantastic results. Do you know what would happen? Immediately those teachers would converge upon you demanding to know the secret to your success! Do you see my point?" (I knew they did not.) The poor teachers harbor illusions that it will be a grading system, or a book, or a video, etc., that will catapult them from mediocrity to merit teaching. But it isn't so, English teachers. Besides there is a personal reason for my not voting yes with you in this matter. It so happens I like the guy and I think he is a very good teacher, at times. I think he has his problems right now — lost the old confidence like Biff Loman in *Death of a Salesman*. Haven't you noticed his hands shaking and the need to either hold coffee or smoke a cigarette? The guy can deliver when he wants to, and I don't believe in telling good teachers how to do their jobs. If my decision seems cowardly, then so be it, I'm sorry. Do what you have to do — I know I will."

They pondered the dilemma for several minutes, but eventually sided with Rebecca. However, they did agree to altering the protest to "some" of us graduate assistants instead of "all" of us graduate assistants. The discussion bothered me for several days, though, and I thought there might be another alternative or a "back-door" approach to the problem of drawing attention to our accepted level of tolerance for oral reports. For instance, we likewise were doing weekly reports in our "Problems In Teaching Composition" from our curriculum advisor, Jan Burns, and each week one of us was to give a forty-five-minute-oral book report about an accepted, noteworthy philosopher on the various teaching modes in education. I felt that I had the luck of the draw by being allowed to choose Ken Macrorie's book, *Uptaught*. I was familiar with his book and acquainted with his provocative, often revolutionary ideas about the teaching of composition. Mr. Macrorie reminded me of a teacher who would not be bound by rules and requirements. To others, I am sure he was considered radical in regards to his opposition to traditional instruction. I liked the man's common-sense-humanitarian approach to teaching. The assignment was one I could definitely get excited about because I planned a rather radical presentation to the report. If the teacher, Jan Burns, rejected the report on the grounds of "showmanship" or "irreverence," then my grade would be in jeopardy for the remainder of the semester. On the other hand, if my plan were successful, I would almost assure myself of an "A" with my teaching demonstration. Also, we were required to write a written report about the book we were orally presenting. I readily identified with Macrorie's thoughts in *Uptaught* and, consequently, I felt more relaxed through the writing of the paper. The day I was scheduled to give my oral report was the following week. I had five days to prepare.

During one of those five days, or at least during the weekend part of it, a departmental party to celebrate Halloween was planned by the Head of the Department at his "bachelor" home. Since I am basically a teetotaler, give or take the one or two "social" drinks, or the occasional drink with dinner, I do not enjoy those parties which primarily center the evening's entertainment around the drinking aspect of the party. Whenever a group needs an excuse for drinking, I usually decline the invitation. I noticed that departmental parties mainly divided into two categories. There were the teas and receptions for the sedate, formal occasions and the boozing bashes for the impromptu-and-any-excuse-you-can-find type of party. The latter I prefer to avoid. However, Stan wrote that he would be in town for the weekend, and he thought it would behoove my good relations with the department to at least make a brief appearance, especially since I had abstained from the Head of the Department's "Jack Daniels Whiskey" party in honor of William Faulkner's birthday at the beginning of the fall term. Stan said that we would arrive at the party about at midpoint in the evening, extend the usual amenities and exit at an honorable, early hour. I was inclined to agree that at this stage of my college career, I could ill afford to have public relations with the department deteriorate to the critical, irreversible point. While I vetoed wearing a Halloween costume bit from want of enthusiasm, I, none the less, agreed that we would pay our respects to all of the higher-ups — be they sober or drunk.

    The boss lived in one of the three or four-family housing areas indicative of small college towns. There are usually the older, quaint, established districts, the close-to-the-university locations, the more modern sections on the fringes of the city, and finally the new housing developments built out in country side environments which offer the benefits of horses, fishing and over-all "natural" living. The boss' home was in the "old guard" section of town. Probably as many as twenty to thirty teachers were located in a two to three-mile section of the city. The boss had an older two-story home. When one entered the hallway and stairway, a visitor could also view the living room adjacent to the entrance way. Anyone could tell immediately that the house was pretty much devoid of feminine decor. Had the wife taken it all when she moved away? There was one couch, one comfortable chair, and the rest of the furniture were straight chairs, possibly borrowed for the occasion. The dining room had the one large dining table and a few scattered dining-room chairs. I saw no plants, nor numerous pictures nor table lamps or bookcases that one would expect in a large home. There were noticeably striking portrait paintings over the fireplace of his three children, but this merely tended to accent the absence of a wife and children within a family home. I found the home to be extremely cold and depressing despite the exterior efforts of the celebration — all and all, I thought the home resembled something occupied by tenants in the border-line poverty level. It was a big disappointment to see the domestic quarters of our Head of the Department. Moreover, I could see that the "tea group" were not in attendance.

By the time we arrived at a respectable hour in the evening, there were several professors and graduate students well on their way to inebriation. In fact, as we entered, we could see four or five guests who were dunking for apples, and from that point on, most "dipped" into the spiked punch bowl or took it straight all evening. I followed the usual protocol and began "mingling" with my Seven-Up well in hand. After about ten minutes, I would have preferred leaving, but Stan was having a "hey-day" visiting old alumni professors. Also, our strategy was for Stan to engage the Head of the Department in a conversation in order to estimate the power of the enemy, so I decided to allow enough time for that to happen.

Since I had, as yet, never felt comfortable in mixing social with business, or in other words of chit-chatting on familiar bases with one's teachers (as this seemed close to unethical conduct), I chose to converse with a graduate student whom I liked but who I could tell was close to being beyond comprehensive conversation. His eyes were blurry, and he no longer tried to "mingle" as did the rest of us. Anyone wishing to visit with Alan Hess had to sit down beside him. I felt real "safe" with good old Alan, even though he was slightly drunk! "Alan," I asked, "you know, I think you would make an excellent teacher." (I honestly did believe it, too.) "You are intelligent, well-read, and you can be dramatic as a Barrymore. With your enthusiastic personality, the 'kids' would follow you anywhere."

"Well, Amy," he drawled, "try telling that to the Education Department because they are the ones who said 'NO' on my practice teaching semester — that's why I am back in graduate school."

For a moment, I was trying to disseminate facts from drunken ramblings, and had to pursue, "I don't understand, Alan, how YOU could not pass the teacher requirements."

Pondering that question and mustering all the soberness he could give to the confusion, he tried to sincerely answer, "Because my block teacher did not approve of my assignments to her students. She had taught the same way (her way) for twenty-some years and won all sorts of honors in every kind of club you want to name, and she made it plain that she did not intend to try any of my 'beginner' methods. But I tried them anyway. Ya know somethin'? I think deep down she was jealous as hell over good old Alan."

Our conversation continued discussing the teaching profession and various comrades within the department, and as Alan warmed with every new drink, he loosened up and proceeded to tell me a bit of departmental gossip.

"See the two talking together over there in the corner?" he slurred with each prospect of news, actually relishing in delight at seeing from a blurred distant at what the world seemed to him: a graying of the clouds.

I turned to see one of our high-ranking (married) professors visiting with one of our graduate assistants. "So, what about it, Alan — there is nothing unusual about that, is there? She's in an office next to mine, and he visits her office every morning at 7:30 a.m. to help her with her composition so she can enter a doctorate program at another university. Maybe it's composition tonight, too, Alan."

"But it wasn't clauses and phrases the other night," he mused at what he held as secret information.

"What are you talking about, Alan?"

"Hey, I *know* what I'm talking about — I'm not that drunk, either. Besides I've got inside information as to what I am talking about."

"Then what are you talking about, Alan?" I asked again.

"It's like this, see. I work at night at the telephone switchboard. You knew that, didn't you?"

"Yes," I replied. "Our mutual friend, Maria, told me because she got a kick out of hearing about the many phone calls the boss put through to Connie. So, what else is new — is there *another* tete-a-tete going on under our nosy noses?"

"Like I'm trying to tell you, Amy. I work at night. Ray works at night, too."

"Who is Ray?"

"Okay, I'm getting there. Ray is my cousin, and he is the night janitor in the English building. He locks up when everyone is out. Now are you following me?"

"Yes, go on. It's beginning to get through to me. Go on, Alan."

"Well, Ray was locking up one night, and he was ready to clean Dr. Hugh Kinney's office when Ray tried the door and found it open. What he found inside, though, was the real shocker. Those two over there (Kinney and Mary Ann) were embraced together."

"Alan, do you have any portion of your brain sober while you are telling me all of this? You've got to be drunk or out of your mind. Are you sure, Alan? Think carefully, one second. Is this really true? You realize that appearances can often be deceiving just like a friendly conversation at a party — us, for instance. One of these guest might think I am trying to seduce you instead of believing we are just good friends who have mutual like and dislikes. We're innocent, but that doesn't stop innuendoes and speculations."

"All I know," said Alan with deliberateness, "is that appearances were not guiltless in this case. Ask Ray if you don't believe me. Just think, a few years ago a person could'va been fired for indiscretions like that."

"If every affair were reported and discipline action followed, there would not be enough faculty to teach, Alan. This is the 'new morality.' "

"Well, anyway, Amy, I thought you might like added fuel to the fire from what I hear about your conflict with the boss."

"Yes, I have about had it with the so-called 'standards of the department.' Thanks for the information, Alan. Who knows but what it might come in handy to use someday. To think that I almost missed this little bash. Let's get our friend Maria and eat out next week. Okay? And, Alan, let Stan and me drive you home or come on with us now so we can see that you get safely home."

"Nah. I haven't even had any vodka yet, and I'm not about to pass up free vodka!"

"All right. So long, old pal, and, Alan, you are welcome to my share of the vodka."

I looked for Stan and found him in conversation with one of his former professors. I nudged his arm which was the signal to say our thank yous and bid adieu. I was excited by what Alan told me, and I was very anxious to discuss with Stan a lot of the old departmental business, and now, the NEW departmental business. Stan was having a wonderful time and was just a little irritated at my wanting to leave.

"Amy, don't you realize that the drinks are free?"

"Nothing in life is free, Stan, and besides you need coffee worse than you need another drink. Let's go to my house for some serious, sober talking."

The evening had moved us along to about eleven o'clock at night, so we went to my house and argued for several more hours into the early morning. The essence of Stan's arguments was that he believed that I was keeping a passive, low-key profile in my school work, in my divorce proceedings and in my social life. At the party, he had sized up the Head of the

Department as a real S.O.B.; and frankly, he had reservations about my being able to do battle, if need be, with such an individual. He said that the boss was the egotistical type of guy who would deal from the bottom and knife from the top if it meant winning. "You thwart an ego as big as his," Stan warned, "and you may not work again."

I told him about the piece of gossip about the "other affair" within the department, and he worried even more. He cautioned me that if I expected moral justice and fairness in an environment such as that, I would have a very rude awakening by the end of the semester. Once we rehashed the dilemma of my many rewrites, we settled on a plan for the remainder of the six weeks of the semester. I was to complete all of the Faulkner assignments, finish the course to get my credit, and to concentrate on rewrites over the Christmas vacation when he would help with the "clean-ups." If I could survive the next six weeks, the suffering would be over. Of course, we, or myself for certain, practically forfeited a much anticipated and needed Christmas vacation. I didn't care what anyone said to the contrary — it wasn't fair to have to deal with the adversity of divorce and college at the same time. Stan thought that the one ace-in-the-hole was to appeal to the Dean of Liberal Arts and Sciences if I did not think I was being given a fair shake within the department. He told me of an incident which occurred several years ago in a language contest where one participating school claimed discriminatory practices. "Just the hint of a discriminatory legal law suit moves mountains in most departments," Stan added. But I had doubts about those possibilities because there was the sixty-year-old graduate assistant in our group who apparently was achieving flying colors in all of her classes. Secretly, I hated her! No, that plan was out. I began thinking ahead to the oral report due Monday and suggested to Stan that we call it a night and finish our talk at Thanksgiving.

Alone in the early hours of morning, I contemplated the night. As a tomboy growing up in a small Midwestern town, the daylight hours meant endless, exhausting hours of tennis, swimming and baseball, and nighttime was the recuperative time before the daybreak's activities would invite me out to play once again; and so it seemed my soul was more kindred to the recreation of the daytime and to the rays of sunshine rather than the blackness of the night. Tonight, I would pull the covers over my head and dream of promises made a long time ago.

The rest of the weekend I prepared for the oral report due Monday in my "Techniques of Composition" class. I was ready and confident — even eager in anticipation of what I was to do. The class met as the last class of the afternoon, so by that time of day most of us graduate assistants had changed into our sports clothes or our everyday-bum-around type of clothes. I chose the sports clothes. When the supervisor called my name, I proceeded to take my chair and place it on top of the two joined seminar tables. I then proceeded to boost myself to the top of the table and from there to the chair where I sat down and commenced giving my oral report. I prefaced my report by saying that out of ALL of the oral reports presented during the semester, I was sure that no one had, as yet, given an oral report on top of the table, so this oral report would at least be different! Laughter ensued, and I could tell from amused expressions and welcome laughter that the class readily accepted the break from the traditional, somnambulant reports. Thus, I continued my report with all of the aplomb and self-confidence of an evangelist converting wayward souls to salvation. The custom after each individual report was to have the supervisor expound upon our subject presented in the report or to follow it up with a mild cross-examination of our material to test our thoroughness and understanding of the subject matter. When I finished, Jan said with a radiant smile, "No comments. Class dismissed."

I knew I had scored and scored big. My colleagues congratulated me and the supervisor later passed on the compliment that the report was excellent! I truly savored the hour. Only one other time in my master's year at that college had I experienced such sweet victory. Life for me was to vacillate between being overly confident and conceited to self-consciousness and filled with self-doubts. Years ago, when my three children were elementary school ages and I was taking them swimming almost every afternoon, I bought me a new bathing suit. With my newly acquired tan and my spindly long legs (and a very pretty suit), I decided that I might just look pretty good in the new suit, so I threw my shoulders back and walked in and out of the pool that day with all of the new-found confidence of a movie star. As we were walking home, which was only two blocks away, one of my kids asked me what that was showing beneath my bathing suit. I looked down, and I discovered that I had forgotten to take off my cotton white underpants! So you see, about the time I tend to become too cocky or overly confident, it seems like someone up above is always there to bring me down. Yet in just about any given circumstances where I care to exert influence — I know that I can emerge the leader — it has happened too many times in my life to say otherwise.

    For example, when I first began my master's program at Southeast Kansas College, I elected to take an anthropology course on "The Plains Indians" as one of my two electives outside of my major field of English. The scheduling and the convenience of the time slot for that course made it possible to take the Indian course and an additional class, a psychology course, as my two summer electives. Our anthropology class met from eight to twelve each morning, Monday through Thursday, for four weeks straight. We were required to present a handmade craft each week using materials that were once available to Plains Indians, submit a two-page written report on that craft and present group reports each week on subjects assigned to us on topics such as religion, dance, myths, crafts, medicine, etc.

    On one assignment, rather than make a craft, I wrote a legend telling about the warring tribes of the two neighboring towns, Caughburg and Wakenda, and how the college town of Caughburg derived its name from a famous Indian battle.

That, too, was well received by the class, and again, I knew instinctively that I had emerged the leader in the class, if I cared to be assertive. It was a fun summer, a great course and a unique professor. He, too, was head of a department — the Sociology Department. The end of the summer was eclipsed by the last hour of the last day of anthropology when the professor concluded his lecture by saying: "I do not usually single out any one individual in the class like this, but I would like to ask Ms. Amy Talbott if she has taught before?"

I said, "Yes, I used to teach in a high school."

He continued, "Well, I imagine your classes must have been most interesting and a lot of fun to take. I have enjoyed your contributions to this class."

To think that I went from that type of eulogy into almost complete rejection from the head of the department in my own field! Little wonder that I found it difficult to accept a restrictive, non-creative atmosphere in, of all fields where one should expect creativity, the English Department. It was beyond understanding to observe how two heads of two departments, so diametrically opposite in application of educational philosophy, could function within the same university. Thank goodness, I had a living, positive testament to my capabilities outside the English Department, or I could not have remained steadfast to the belief in my own individualistic potential. Since it is always much easier managing and manipulating people who will stay within the norm or the prescribed boundaries, administration will continue to build around a nucleus of safe "yes" people and reward the "no" or "maybe so" people only if there is a mandate by the populous. One sees this happen frequently in areas of music, drama or coaching where the teacher or coach may be controversial and difficult for the administration to control, but because of the popular student demands for the teacher's talents, administration will begrudgingly, and most quietly, capitulate to the teacher's idiosyncrasies. Great administrators do NOT feel threatened by dynamic teachers, but rather instead, they know how to use those talents to their own benefit. Like Frank

Kapra, the famous movie director once said: "Genius is knowing when to get the hell out of the way and let the actors do their stuff." Sometimes genius in teaching is knowing when to become part of the audience, and genius in administration is knowing when to let the actors do their stuff!! I did not believe the Head of the English Department was by any means a genius, nor could I any longer expect "star" treatment. My theater was in the trenches of teaching, and I was just about ready to emerge for the final offensive assault for the end of the semester.

Shortly after the Halloween party, I received a letter from the Dean of the Graduate Office congratulating me on being selected to receive the Pennington Fellowship of Southeast Kansas College. I dismissed the letter as probably belonging to one of the honorary societies which for $15 one could join and become a lifelong member. I guessed that all of the graduate assistants in the English Department had received a similar letter. When I was reading it to Greg Hudson, with whom I shared an office, I asked if he had received one, too. "No, I didn't get one, but I wish I had because it would look great on my transcript. Sounds real important, Amy. You better check into it."

So I made inquiries around the department to find out what the Pennington Fellowship was and to find out why I was singled out as a recipient. The general consensus was that it was an honor and only two of us English graduate assistants were chosen. Finally, my supervisor said that the $4,000 Fellowship grants were provided by an endowment fund from the Pennington family and were awarded annually to deserving graduate students. What it all amounted to in monetary results was that my $400 a month pay for teaching one course in freshmen composition was being paid, and had been paid, for several months from the Pennington Endowment Fund. Before I could fully comprehend that it was I who was singled out to receive that award, I had to be told that the two of us were invited, along with fellowship recipients from the other departments, to a school luncheon with the President of the college, the assistant President and the Dean of Graduate School. If that were not enough to put me in shock, the following day I received a letter from the Head of the English Department congratulating me and informing me of a reception that would be held at Professor Kinney's home in honor of Peggy Bruner and myself receiving the English Department's fellowships. I was astounded. I had mixed emotions, too. Part of me felt embarrassed and ashamed of my poor showing in the Faulkner class which now seemed all the more incongruent with the award; and still, part of me wanted to bask in the accolade of the moment. I needed that honor immensely. My colleagues rallied around the event as if to lend support to what I am sure all knew to be a most discouraging semester for me. Even two of the graduate assistants, living out of the city, made a special effort to return again that evening for the party. I was entering a professor's home for the second time that semester.

Professor Kinney's house was in the same district as the Head of the English Department's house. Professor Kinney's home, like the boss' home, was an older, two-story house, but more typical of what one would expect a professor's home to be. The furniture was ornate and antique. Within the home was the expected large study lined with shelves of hundreds of books, an elegant dining room, a cozy living-room fireplace with warm, attractive oriental rugs on beautiful hardwood floors. I looked for signs which reflected an unhappy household or a divided household, but I saw none. Perhaps the rumors of his involvement with Mary Ann were erroneous after all, or maybe he was only enjoying a middle-age flirtation with a younger woman — nothing more. However, I rather doubted that they would sit together in a secluded corner at this party.

The two parties I had thus far attended were entirely opposite in character. More of the older, conservative, family-oriented English faculty were there as well as the President of the College, the assistant President and their wives. Everything and everyone culminated into a warm, cordial "mixer."

No one was "potted" and good conversation prevailed over the necessities of drinking, although drinks were optional with the tasteful buffet. That night, with that particular crowd, punch was the more popular drink. I will not forget seeing the assistant President and several others seated on the rug in jovial discussion with as many as could possibly cluster around the animated assistant President. I had witnessed another side of the academia, and I liked what I saw. I began to feel for the first time that semester that there might be a hereafter after I was finished with my Masters. For the moment, I could pretend that there were no more obstacles ahead, nor was there any reason to let one man and one class detract from what was obviously Peggy's and my evening! I now had two aces in the hole in case I did not manage to escape my Faulkner class with a passing grade.

Most of our classes were now coasting toward the first-semester finals by the first week of December. The main social parties were all over, and the tempo had to changed to serious finality. Our Faulkner class had dwindled to three people ever since the Thanksgiving vacation, two of which were graduate assistants, myself included, and one was the editor of the college newspaper.

I asked the editor what he was going to write about for his last paper, and he disclosed that he hadn't the slightest idea because everything he wrote was returned with NOT ACCEPTABLE, so he said that he couldn't seem to please the professor with anything he wrote. Gradually the editor quit coming to class our last three weeks, and that left two of us to carry the burden of discussion during those weeks.

Two weeks before our last meeting, I was planning to skip out and meet a friend for coffee from my hometown who was also in a night course at a similar time as mine. My conscience got the better of me, however, because I could not leave the one girl to carry the tedious load of discussion all by herself. As for my last researched paper, I had wanted to write on (and had already researched considerable material about) how there could be a screen adaptation of *Absalom Absalom*. The boss said that *Absalom Absalom* could never be made into a movie, so I decided not to try for any more "left-wing creativity." I still believe a very good script could be written about *Absalom Absalom* by following themes — not fact-by-fact plots. The theme of the essence of a power-driven, self-made-genius man tainted with the corruption of money and miscegenation could be a Southern saga similar to *Beulah Land,* etc. It certainly invites more promise for development than the current television adapted sagas such as *Lace, Master of the Game* and *The Thorn Birds.* To play it safe, though, I wrote about the book I was doing as an oral report, *As I Lay Dying* (no pun of coincidence intended).

Again, I was not enthused with the paper nor inspired. I tried for straight critical analysis-research writing, with no frills nor any subjective intrusions. On the last evening of our semester Faulkner class, I took my ten-page paper to class, my home-baked cookies to class, the Christmas plates and napkins, and the three of us (two students and one teacher) held class. I truly made every effort, I thought, at conciliatory remarks. I asked the boss if he would like for me to pick another theme for my five-page paper on *Light In August,* or where did he think I went so wrong on that paper? He said that it was not that bad of a paper — I just needed to "clean it up" by giving more specific examples when I referred to my own interpretations of the novel and to make the corrections he had marked on the paper. I said that I would and that I hoped to have it all finished during the holidays. He nodded in agreement and said "fine." We dismissed class on the "Merry Christmas" good nights to one another. That was one week before Christmas. The course had ended without one grade issued the whole semester. I had come to class sixteen straight weeks without knowing what I could expect as a final grade in the course.

The week after Christmas, I received my grades with a "C" in Faulkner, a "B" in "Men, Women and Love In Literature," an "incomplete" in my modern British novel class, and an "A" in my Techniques of Composition class. I went into deep depression. For two days I got out of bed only to eat and to walk the dog and to watch television. For all I knew, I could not have a "C" on my transcript on the graduate level. Stan was home for Christmas vacation, so I sent out an S.O.S to him with the added postscript that the pencil was too heavy of a burden to lift, let alone accomplish the impossible task of rewriting. Stan argued that I had to do it and that I could not go in and confront the boss about my grade without first having some of my work to show him which indicated that I was sincere in wanting to revise the papers. He said he would help me correct the six individual reports, but before we went to all of the trouble to do additional research and rewrite to the five-page paper, I should first ask the boss if there were any possibility of getting my grade changed from a "C" to a "B?" If the boss agreed to changing the grade, Stan and I would redouble our efforts on the more difficult five-page paper.

For two wintry, late December days, we worked on the reports, and for two evenings I neatly typed them to near perfection. I prided myself on my careful, measured, neat typing. When my husband was going to school in Manhattan, right after we were first married, I worked as a secretary for the Head of the Horticulture Department at Kansas State University. But that was another story about another Head of the Department. Anyway, after the reports were typed, I decided to let the New Year's holidays pass before attempting to find anyone at work back in the English Department. Finally, about one week before we were to begin the spring semester and were due back for more in-service training, I took my papers up to the fourth floor of the English Department and asked the secretary for an interview with the boss. I kept breathing deeply in order not to feel panicky and to make sure my voice was strong, resonant and vibrant. I had sung to myself off and on for several hours prior to arriving at the college in order to ensure extra strength to my voice. Nevertheless, I could not force back the same uncontrollable inadequacies I was prone to experience in the presence of authoritative cross examinations, nor had the divorce during the past year lessened any of those inadequacies. I had yet to recover from the recent ordeal of finding out what it was like to have to sit in a courtroom and listen to the judge and the lawyers determine one's dignity and worth. It was a denigrating, demoralizing experience I hope never to repeat.

As my name was called by the boss' secretary, I took a deep, deep breath and told myself I had come this far, and I would not be stopped from the chance to have a good job and to begin a new life for myself. In a sense, I had already experienced about the whole bagful of disappointments in two short years, and I had nowhere to go but forward. I threw my head back and strode into the office. "Dr. Shadden, I want to submit to you my six rewritten reports."

"I thought that you understood that everything had to be completed by the end of the course, Amy."

"No, sir," I replied. "I did not understand that, Dr. Shadden. I said to you in our last class meeting that I would get all of my rewritten work completed during the Christmas vacation, and you acknowledged that."

"I don't remember that," he added.

"Does this mean that I am going to have to take an additional course in order to meet the Master's requirements?"

"Oh, no," he said. "You can have a 'C' on your record as long as you can average that 'C' with your other grades to maintain a 3.0 average."

"But, Dr. Shadden, isn't there any way I can raise my grade if I redo all of my work?"

He hesitated for a brief moment before answering, "What you probably need for me to do is to change your grade to incomplete, right?"

"Yes, that would help, Dr. Shadden." I left his office with the understanding that I would receive an "incomplete" in Faulkner, rather than the "C," and that with continued diligence to rewrites, I could expect to see my grade raised to that of a "B." I felt optimistic about those possibilities.

As for my incomplete in the Modern British Novel, I did not overly concern myself about it because the incomplete was not due to having not completed my class assignments, but from misunderstanding the instructor's format for a research paper due during the last week of the course. For example, rather than to research what was happening in the author's life the year the novel I was researching was published, we were to research the origins of the beginning of the creative process by that author for the writing of that particular novel. Whatever I had to redo for that paper had very little to do with the learning process. To merely exchange facts from one paper to another, I considered redundant and repetitious and a mere formality, all of which was time-consuming on my dwindling so-called Christmas vacation. A wiser teacher would have said that I already demonstrated the techniques of research in addition to indicating a knowledge of my subject matter, and I could submit a small report on the added information. But he didn't. I guessed that I was between an "A" or "B" at the time in that course, so I elected to try to please in every way possible. As it turned out later, I could not tell that the rewrite of the paper had affected my grade in the least. However, like a true athletic competitor, I decided since I was so close to the "A" as my final grade, that I would "go for it."

From a logical process and elimination observation during the semester, I deduced that I could have a "superior" final by covering the thrust of the thematic content of all of our novels for the final rather than the two or three suggested by the Modern British Novel instructor. I based that definitive reasoning on the obvious performance of our weekly discussion sessions where it was apparent that a "majority" of the class did not read the novels, had no intention of reading the novels, and what was more, cared less if it was a novel. But that did not seem to matter in the final analysis of the semester final, and so I had wrongly "second guessed" a professor for the second time in the semester! Didn't John Lennon aptly write that "Nobody told me there would be days like this." Similarly, I began to see that the background music for my entire semester of melodramatic study, with all of its boos, hisses and cheers, and the gamut of emotions, was music reminiscent of Class B movies, or those movies attempting a form of realism technique by playing continual music throughout the dialogue and action, and that music was infamously familiar by its arrangements of xylophone solos alternating with the trumpet solos. Anytime I see an old "B" movie on TV with background trumpet and xylophone music, I instantly turn channels because I know the movie is a "B" drama, "B" music, "B" producing and "B" directing and "B" acting. Literary people might see a touch of the irony in my struggle to evaluate myself by the standards of "B" movies. So be it!

As for my "B" in "Men, Women and Love in Literature," that was a laugh! I had met some classmates from that class at a shopping mall during Christmas vacation, and they inquired about what my final grade was in the course? When I said, "B," they could not believe it. One girl said, "I thought that you of all people would have an "A" out of the course, but I hear he gave about everyone "B's" and "C's." That was the class in which so many of the graduate assistants had complained about all of the group reports inflicted upon us without guidance or teaching from the instructor. To be singled out as "you of all people should get an "A," reinforced what I knew to be true, that I had given one of the best oral reports from the graduate assistants. When I was through with my oral report, the class clapped, and like the anthropology class, I had about a half-dozen students come up afterwards and congratulate me on the report and ask me if I were a teacher or had I taught before? I knew at the time that the report was good — I knew it in my bones! One does not have to teach five or ten years to know instinctively when he or she has reached an audience. I understand college professors must periodically publish either researched, scholarly papers in their field, or publish creative papers in the fields of poetry, literature, music and drama. Presently, this is considered erudite and helps distinguish the college teachers from the "other" teachers. I think more would be achieved as a contribution to higher education if some of the college professors would write on topics such as: "How to Solve Forty-five Minutes of Ennui Out of the Fifty-five Minutes," or "How to Have a Successful Class with Only Two Students after Eight Others Dropped Out," or "How to Have Students Leave a Classroom with a Happy, Satisfied Feeling."

When my twelve-page paper in "Men, Women and Love in Literature" was returned with an "A" and the remark, "I enjoyed your paper," I could only surmise that it was my final that was poor and was the cause of my "B." Ashamedly, I, nevertheless, suspected that those who complained to the instructor about the quantity and quality of the many oral reports probably got the "A's" (for I have seen it happen before), or else those who had found out that if one "entertained" the professor, one's grade would improve and would likewise score the "A's." My mentor back in a junior college had told me of a true story of another student taking one of Dr. Whitney's classes. She had the mentor teacher read her term paper and proceeded to ask her what she thought of the final work. The paper had an "A" on it, and she had an "A" from the course. "Why, Janice, this is a terrible paper," the older teacher said to her.

Janice laughed and said, "I know it is."

"Well, then why did you get an 'A' on the paper and an 'A' in the course?"

"Because he likes to come over and share a couple of beers."

That was but one of the many stories circulated about the legendary, twice-divorced Dr. Whitney. His current reputation was less glamorous than in his hey-days of the '70s. One graduate assistant told me that several weeks before the end of the semester, she asked him why he did the disco-bar scene every night, and he answered by saying, "Because I am lonely." Aren't we all!!!

I stayed in bed some nights and from the dark I watched what little traffic there was go by my street. Professor Whitney even lived two blocks from me, and many times I watched out the window, from the dark of the room where I could not be seen and secretly hoped he might "drop by." Once he did stop by in the daytime to admire my cycle and suggested we take a ride. As Stan said, "You are certainly not the 'typical' divorced woman. I figured that had I made any type of friendly overture, we would have been seeing one another. But I was afraid, afraid that he was too much like my "ex," and I was afraid to begin again or to take a chance upon rejection. Rejection can take an ugly, destructive path if allowed to run rampant without any direction or spiritual affirmation to believe otherwise. Yes, it was easier to remain at home, in the dark, in seclusion, and to hibernate. After all, how many times in one's life does a knight in shining armor ride by? And if he did come along, would I be sitting in the dark and not know that he was passing? Tomorrow I would begin rewriting my paper.

There remained one more week left in the vacation before the beginning of the spring semester. I was going to make the deadline with my rewritten Faulkner paper about two days before the new spring semester. Plus, I had rewritten the paper for the Modern British Novel course which would correct the incomplete in that course, too. When I left the paper with Dr. Kinney, he assured me that the "incomplete" would be taken off my record. One paper down and one to go!

Finally, after deletions, inserts and added research, I had repaired and revised my Faulkner paper. Again, I approached the secretary to ask for an appointment to see the Head of the Department. That secretary had a way of making one feel like it was a January day even if the day was in July. Some school secretaries seem to think that they are not working for the public; and, therefore, any interruption in their daily schedule is an affront to the wheels of progress grinding slowly in their electric typewriters. (A few words more on the subject of secretaries, later.) After a decent interval of waiting, the secretary motioned for me to go on in to the boss' office.

"Dr. Shadden, I wish to submit my corrected paper on *Light In August*."

"Amy," he greeted me without enthusiasm, "I have decided

to let the grade stand as is" (which was a "C").

I sat down quickly for I felt like someone had hit me across the knees with a two-by-four. "But, Dr. Shadden, you said that you would change the grade to incomplete — that is why I took the time to rewrite this paper."

"Well, I do not recall having that understanding. All work must be completed before the last day of a course unless you inform the instructor you wish to take an incomplete."

"I know that now, Dr. Shadden, and I will admit I was naive in not finding out more of my responsibilities much sooner. I am sorry. Please do not take this as an excuse, but you know ten years ago when I was going to college here, I was receiving compliments for my writing from the head of the English department at that time, plus several other professors, too. I realize that styles have changed and that I am rusty in some areas of writing, but, Dr. Shadden, I have faithfully met all of the requirements you have requested. Frankly, I do not believe I would want a "C" writer teaching my freshman composition."

"No, that is not so, Amy. If Jan Burns says you have an "A" in your teaching, I do not question her evaluation. If Dr. Kinney says that you have a "B" in Modern British Novel, I do not question his grade. Please understand that the Faulkner class is most difficult, and I personally felt that you did "C" work in the course, and that is why I will let the grade stand."

"All right, Dr. Shadden, I do not intend to argue this point with you, but I do wish you to know that I think this action is very unfair. The last three weeks of the class there were only two of us to carry the load of the discussion out of what was originally a class of eight. The discussion load was most difficult."

"Oh, I realize that, but my decision is still the same."

"Then we have nothing more to discuss. Thank you for seeing me. Good Day."

I wanted to run and put the Faulkner paper in the first trash can I could find, but I thought better of that vengeful act. I guess I wanted to keep the paper forever to remind me of an unbelievable event in my college career.

I had less that forty-eight hours to decide whether I could take another semester of "game playing." I expected my second semester (the spring semester) to be much easier than the fall one, and, of course, without any more classes from the Head of the Department. I could not afford to consider one negative thought such as quitting school. Yet this was one of those times that I wished I liked to drink because I sure felt like tying one on — anything to be totally bombed out and to be able to forget what had just happened. Instead, I called Stan long distance once more and told him about my meeting with Dr. Shadden. He said to meet him in Wakenda tomorrow because it was very important and to be sure not to do anything dumb like quitting school, running away or telling someone off. He reminded me that there were other choices and that he had some very good advice for me. (Everyone has good advice.) I had never had to buy insurance, figure income taxes, keep records, worry about the car or health insurance, but lately I could tell I was painfully evolving toward the need to take charge of my own life. I went to Wakenda the next day to listen to more advice.

For one thing, Stan thought I should go back to the boss and ask that he specifically point out what errors I was making in my writing, or at least ask him to explain, point by point, the basis for his dissatisfaction with my work. Stan said I needed to have an explicit understanding with Dr. Shadden regarding his grading, not only for my own satisfaction, but also in case I decided to appeal his decision to the Dean of Liberal Arts and Sciences. Stan concluded that should be my next move. Also, Stan interpreted the actions of the Head of the Department as a possible bad omen for my completing my master's exams in the summer. Stan effusively argued that if I did not more or less protest the treatment that I had received in the English Department, that I invited the situation to continue, thereby jeopardizing my chances for fair rhetorical plea. Stan placed on my shoulders the burden of the whole human race and what I owed to other innocent, unsuspecting English majors who would be unfortunate to follow in my footsteps. To add to the humanitarian need for action, Stan exhorted me to realize that, more importantly, I owed it to the college to inform them of unprofessional antics happening within the English Department as well as the questioning of the necessity of having a paid instructor for a class of three!

I listened and absorbed all of the persuasive arguments, but mainly those arguments were not within the framework of my own practiced philosophy. I do not believe "vendettas" (or trying to equalize the score) often work to the advantage of the well-intentioned individual. It is better to fight for what you believe in rather than to fight against what others believe. I knew myself not to be guilty to most of the ridiculous grading criticisms and not guilty to any unscrupulous, immoral behaviors, so why would it be necessary to wage a crusade against the department? Besides, I reasoned that a common layman or mere student does not need to tell a college how to manage their own department. Logically, I assumed that they, above everyone else, were aware that they were paying for an instructor to teach a semester class of three, one of whom failed the course out of the three students. Even if there is questionable activity within a school, usually decisions affecting future changes are based on administrative interpretations, not student interpretations. "Higher-ups" tend to dismiss student requests. If nothing else, I have learned through experience in business and in teaching that even where there are wrongs pointed out, the employer closes ranks and rarely takes immediate or drastic action against his employees; and frankly, that is the way it should be unless the wrong includes something serious as a felony or a misdemeanor within the business. Also, if the bone of contention is what is believed to be "singular" in protest, the individual is dismissed as "radical," "hard-to-get-along-with" or a "trouble maker." I have seen schools take five years or more for a board of education to accumulate enough damaging evidence to indict a principal or a teacher. In Wakenda, the local high school took ten years and two courtroom hearings to dismiss two teachers on the grounds of what the board considered lack of classroom discipline.

What adds to the comedy of errors of attempting to define a merit teacher is the repeated practice of relating discipline to good teaching. By that logic, one can place a muscular man or coach in a classroom and create a quiet environment but an atmosphere devoid of creativity or individuality. Often progress in education is two steps forward and one backward, and by the time education has interpreted the "sign of the times," another social upheaval promulgates a complexity of political, social and economic problems within the framework of our educational system. What echoes through the universities in loud obscenities in one decade may be a silent epitaph to another decade. Can school boards recognize these changes without ever being in a classroom? Do they visit with the teachers who are close to these changes?

Stan could not have disagreed more with my decision not to appeal Dr. Shadden's decision about my grade. He said that I was a pacifist and a masochist, and I accused him of showing off with his rhetoric in front of several others, and soon we were at shouting level with one another. We were both out of control, so I excused myself since I had also reached the point of cry-baby tears. I told him that I had just finished twenty-eight years of having someone assiduously attack me verbally like that and enough was enough. I recognized by the end of the argument that I was, for the first time, on my own and in complete control of all of my decisions, even if they were unwise or futile.

Whatever I chose to do had to reflect what I now was and what I hoped to be as an individual struggling for her own autonomy for the future. I knew other women who had crusaded against inequities within the social system, but I was not a crusader. I welcomed a cause to be dedicated to someday, but I did not know which cause to join. I envied others who were so enthusiastically caught up in a cause or a religion that infused them with endless energy and creativity. I was an idealist who believed in the Protestant ethic in which we live by example and we persuade and lead others to rightness, not drive them to the cause. I had faith that God was in charge of my life, and he would choose the path I was to lead or to follow, whether that plan be to my liking or not. Barring no divine intervention to direct me elsewhere, I had less than twenty-four hours to decide for myself whether to finish out the year.

1949

In my hometown, we used to have three theaters on our Main Street. Our population was about ten thousand in the 1940s. Now our population is about nine thousand, and presently we have no theaters in town due to economic restraints. My dad managed a grocery store which stayed open until nine-thirty Saturday nights, so by the time he could clear the store of all late shoppers, have the boys sweep the floors with red sawdust and check the cash registers, the hour would be about 10:30 p.m. before he was ready to lock the doors to conclude the long, long day. Since we needed to share the one family car, we needed either to meet my dad after the store closed late Saturday night or to let Dad take the car back with him after his Saturday noon hour, if he took time to come home for lunch. Because Saturdays were the big days for town merchants, most generally he ate a short lunch at one of the three or four convenient diners. Most of the time, we kept the car for errands and shopping and taking in an evening double feature at one of the theaters. By that time, Dad was ready to go home, and so were we. About every Saturday, I went to the matinee (usually one cowboy picture and one drama or comedy), and then I went to the same show that evening, plus on Sundays I went to another show in the afternoons. That was entertainment! I was a real movie buff — one of those fans who plastered the bedroom wall-to-wall with movie stars' pictures! I knew every star's name, their mate, and every movie they had starred in for the last ten years. Part of the Saturday's entertainment, when we kept the car, would be to go up town late Saturday afternoon in order to be among the first to get a place to park to watch the people go by. People walked the streets, kind of like the old-fashioned promenades, three or four abreast, and the spectacle was literally a parade of people coming to town to celebrate Saturday night. Traffic was two lanes, and cars would drive up and down the streets either trying to park or simply enjoying the parade by watching from the car. Rarely did one find a place to park on the first try down Main Street, not unless one got there between afternoon shopping and evening shopping. Ordinarily we timed the parking early enough to have one of the better sightseeing positions and late enough to allow us time to buy the Saturday supper special of hamburgers, fries and malts. Before the fast-food era, one local restaurant fried the hamburgers and thread-like onions together and, thus, produced a quality of taste unequaled today.

My sister and I invariably got tired of listening to the grown-ups visit at the cars or in the stores, so we would haunt the drugstores reading comic books, and if we had had a generous week in our household chores, rewarded by an allowance, we had enough for a soda or a "400" or a strawberry phosphate. A "400" was a four-inch glass of milk, chocolate, carbonated water and crushed ice, and the crushed ice in the drink was what gave the drink its eternal fame. Sodas were something one enjoyed best on Sundays or after school. But mostly, I saved my money for the double features and for the treats sold at the show. I suppose I squandered a fortune on "black crows" or "jujubes." In all of those many excursions to town, the show and the drugstore, I never considered whether to question why the blacks did not promenade the streets, too, or go in the drugstores to meet the gang for a soda. I accepted, without question, that they were supposed to sit in the balcony at the shows in what was derogatorily termed "nigger heaven." The times that we walked to town from the east side to the west side, we had to cross a section of the colored town which ran about one mile north and one mile south. The sidewalk took us under the railroad bridge, and if we continued a short distance west, we would turn north about a half block to enter the blacks "honky-tonk" section. If we turned south, we entered the rows of shanty houses the townspeople called "Jordan's Row."

We were never to walk home alone at night, not that we cared to, because in all truthfulness most of us were scared to death to walk under the bridge at night. All sorts of surreptitious tales circulated as to what went on in Jordan's Row, and that kept us as much in line as did the rubber hose tales in our grade school on the east side. Even in the daytime, and if one were young and he had to walk home from town or school, he increased his walking tempo tremendously. Those less brave took another route which did not intersect Jordan's Row. I truly believed as a child that blacks were different, and it never occurred to me to believe that they should share our facilities. Now that type of innocence both depresses and scares me to think that I never questioned racial segregation then. There was a city bus, too, and if we did not take advantage of the bus to get back and forth to town, we utilized it for "joy rides" and a chance to meet our friends, both girls and boys, and exchange news. Blacks, of course, were to sit at the back, and that, too, seemed quite natural to me. The blacks had their own swimming pool out in the far northwest side of town. On the bus, I was fascinated by black mannerisms and by their dress and talk, believing all of the time that they were supposed to talk with the subjugated "yessah," "noosah" boss dialect. They seemed to laugh by loud, silly giggles and talk loudly when spoken to, but, of course, I was seeing a race unaccustomed to identification on a human level, and what I interpreted as a novelty, clownish behavior was, indeed, the freakish, imposed behavior relegated to them by the white population.

Characteristic of many small towns, we had our "crazies" or oddities we pursued with confused curiosity if left to our own adventures. The town black "crazy" rode a bike with an antenna on it and a license plate on the back of the seat because he believed the bike to be his automobile. The town white "crazy," who also rode a bike and talked to it while delivering papers, and who was, according to the white population, merely "touched" or shell-shocked from World War I. If his bike tipped over, which it did all of the time, he would heap continual blasphemies at it for ten or fifteen minutes for its failure to propel him upright and forward. If our mothers knew when one of those spells was coming on, we were ushered inside immediately. My dad used to buy him meals at a local diner and see that he had a warm coat and decent shoes in which to earn a little money selling papers. Both races had their rejects, but the white race had a way of glorifying even the lowliest of unsavory citizens. I suppose our small town was not too dissimilar from other small towns of the period. We were poor in equal rights and rich in family living. We had our share of hoboes and tramps riding the rails from one town to another, and we had our share of scandals on both sides of the railroad tracks. Small towns notoriously keep a tidy house by sweeping the dirt either out the back door or under the rug for fall, winter, spring and summer. Therein lies many a buried scandal beneath a layer or two of dirt!

• • • • • • • •
1982
• • • • • • • •

I could hear the campus chimes playing the theme from *Doctor Zhivago*, and I quickened my steps to arrive early for my first day of teaching for the spring semester. As yet, there was no traffic on campus, so there was an early-morning solitude and stillness which quieted the first-day jitters and butterflies that I always experienced for opening day. I planned for the first day of school to slip in to class rather early and sit with the students while they waited for a teacher to arrive. We were to have all new students, so I gambled that I could go incognito with the crowd and appear relatively unnoticed at a student desk while I, too, waited with the students for the appearance of a teacher. I received a few inquisitive glances, but actually older students were no special novelty in college, and besides, the students were mainly caught up in finding both the right room and looking for the right buddy. After a decent interval of waiting for a teacher to appear, a number of student voices began murmuring and speculating as to whether they really were in the right room or if a teacher had been assigned. No doubt many students anxiously waited for several more minutes to pass so that they could legally leave, and a few gave me closer scrutiny. I decided that the time was ripe. I got out of my chair and began my first day of teaching:

Good morning, ladies and gentlemen. I am your English 102 teacher, and I have traded places with you for a few short minutes to see what it was like to be out there with you. It is terrifying, isn't it? If there comes a time during the semester when you would like to trade places with me, I invite you to feel free to do so because I sincerely hope that the semester does not end without my learning just as much from you as you will from — perhaps more, and I hope you will equally learn from one another. Then, we will have a successful class indeed. Let us begin.

• • • • • • • •
1983-1984
• • • • • • • •

REFLECTIONS OF A SUBSTITUTE TEACHER

The following incidents are true and all happened within a thirty-mile radius during my one year as a substitute teacher while waiting for a full-time position which would allow me to stay in Wakenda:

After I received my master's degree in the summer of 1983 at Southeast Kansas College, the thought never entered my mind that I would move into the fall of the year unemployed — just like the thoughts never occurred to me to question racial segregation during the 1940s. I kept saying over and over to myself, "I can't believe that I am unemployed — I just can't believe it." At the time of the spring hiring, I had had my eye on three potential English jobs in my hometown, and that was where I preferred to keep my roots. Unless I was fortunate enough to secure a college position within a hundred-mile radius, I had pretty much decided that I would settle only on a local job, either high school or middle school.

In August, as the opening day for school approached, I began to realize that there would definitely not be two English positions available; there was still a very good possibility that the third English opening would materialize even as late as into the second and third weeks of school. In fact, the superintendent encouragingly assured me to "hang on" and be ready to move into the position as soon as word was received that a particular high school English teacher would move from her teaching position into an administrative position in another city. But that never happened. Her job, which was to be a newly created administrative office, was vetoed for at least the remainder of the fiscal school. From that point on, I became unemployed, and the only alternative (other than to go back to grocery clerking which I did the following year) to employment was to accept substitute employment, or in other words, become the scourge of the school, the bane of the teaching profession, the lowest form in the teaching evolution, and the wild game target for the species of students who live for the hunt and the kill of substitute teachers. And, thus, I began.

Most teachers provide busy work for substitute teachers. A few of the assignments are more valuable than others. One can always tell by how seriously the students tackle their work how valued the busy work really is. Once a teacher I substituted for was so vague in her directions and instructions for what I was to do the entire day, that I spent the good part of the morning trying to find everything. Therefore, I decided that in my end-of-the-day report to leave her the following explanation: "Everyone did his/her homework as assigned except the girl in the blue jeans and tennis shoes."

· · · · · · · ·

My second week of substitute teaching, I was assigned the notorious task of substituting in the middle school band which had the bountiful supply of musicians ranging from eighty to one hundred members in each of the three grades. The principal pulled me aside and warned me that they (the band) had had lots of trouble with substitutes in band. He added, as what was no doubt meant to be comfort and reassurance, "If you have any trouble with some who do not cooperate, send them to me, and I will take care of them." With that thought in mind, I moved ever forward with rededication and determination that I would not only substitute in band, but that I would also lead the band!! After all, I knew a little bit of music and had played in a school band some six years while going to school through junior high and high school. Directing the band, however, was an opportunity I could not pass up.

I grasped the baton (which I later learned was the cleaning rod for a flute) and, believe it or not, managed to get the band started on the same march at the same time. I was ecstatic! I did not attempt to try to read the music since it was all I could do to watch that they were following along and that I was in time with them, too. About halfway through the march, I suddenly realized I would not know when the march would end. I could start them — I could not stop them! I would have to fake it with a little theatrical antics. But isn't that what a lot of teaching is? Very good dramatic acting? Out of the approximately eighty-some members in the band, five or six were floating around the entire time we were playing the marches. In the "good old days," we band musicians could NOT leave our seats until the band period was over. I finally stopped the band and asked why those half-dozen were not in their seats playing their instruments with the rest of us? They said that there was not enough music or instruments for everyone to play, so they always "stroll." The answer left me very little choice but to continue the procedure. When the period was about over, the shy little girl in the front asked if she could please have her cleaning rod back for her flute? By the end of the day, I felt that I had met one more insurmountable obstacle head on — fought the good race and won. Surely I would care not to repeat the performance day after day. Directing a band is undoubtedly for the very young, very stout, very patient, and for those whose musical tastes beat to the same drummer. Bless all music teachers!!

•••••••••

One day at a middle school, I was substituting in seventh-grade English, and on that particular day many of the students were returning their "progress reports." Under each subject of the progress report, the student was to evaluate his own grades and likewise evaluate his own progress in that subject. I glanced at several of the reports, and one of the reports in particular caught my attention, for it read: "I thought I would do pretty good in English. I don't know what went wrong." That really seemed prophetically honest and seemed to epitomize the classroom dilemma of a "poor performance" student. If he knew what was wrong, then naturally he would be able not to repeat his infractions time after time. I doubted whether the parents, or the teacher, or the administration glanced twice at the student's perception about his own problems of learning, but in his locked, groping, child-like mind, he had innately understood what supposedly wise, intelligent adults failed to identify. Would his whole year continue in the same innocent frustration?

•••••••••

Sometimes I like to greet a class with the tone of horseshack on "Welcome Back Cotter," and say, "H-e-l-l-o and how are you?" or mimic the dialogue and the mood of Richard Pryor and Gene Wilder in *Stir Crazy* when they shuffle off to jail and are saying, "We're bad ... we're bad."

•••••••••

In some high schools, after students have received their daily assignments and have completed them, most of the students want teachers to call in to the office and request that the office turn on a certain radio station — not country/

western, not the local "slow station — but rock music. If a substitute teacher has some of the "personality classes," she can "tease" them for awhile and acknowledge their request for music by immediately singing for them, or what will really cause instant flak is to call in requesting Lawrence Welk music.

• • • • • • • •

If we set up the hypothesis that: the high school averages three substitutes a month who average being paid $450 a month, we have the average substitute expenditure of $1350 a month, and sum times that amount by nine months, we have the annual expenditure of $12,250 for the minimum cost of a substitute teacher. Therefore, why not dismiss the classes to a commons area, which easily accommodates several hundred people, when a teacher is unable to report to work, and hire a paraprofessional at approximately $6,000 a year to supervise the commons area, distribute any of the assignments, take roll, and watch for any rowdiness or misbehavior from students during that hour. This would accomplish a two-fold purpose: (1) Substitute teachers and students would not need to endure what is obvious to both teacher and student: BUSYWORK. (2) In classroom and shops where expensive or dangerous equipment is in use, there is always a high degree of risk under the conditions where "the cat's away and the mice will play." But by sending the students to the commons area, in preference to staying in the classroom, the school can protect the expensive equipment from careless operation, possibly even vandalism. This method of substituting for substitutes could save the school district $6,000 a year, and more, in the high school alone. That saving could be wisely appropriated for the purchase of much needed technological equipment. Even funneling money back to teachers' salaries for a portion of the sick days they did not need to take, would provide an additional attendance incentive under this system. Perhaps all concerned would be happier. Naturally, such a system would be too relaxed, too unstructured for schools below the high school level.

• • • • • • • •

Substituting for English and history teachers requires more perseverance and patience than any of the other subjects. The reason for this is that their favorite assignments are to ask the substitutes to tell the students to answer the questions at the back of the chapter or do the vocabulary at the end of the chapter, and when they are finished, read the next chapter. That is like parents telling a babysitter to have the children clean their room, and when they are finished, lie down and take a nap. Both directions have the same nerve-wrecking results for the one who is "babysitting."

One English teacher, whom I substituted for, told me to have the students to write an essay (with three supports) on the following topic: "If I were free to travel down the road, I would choose to go to_____." About five minutes later, the first paper was handed in, leaving that student unoccupied for the next fifty minutes! Several minutes later, two or three more students' papers were handed in, and so I began trying to persuade them that I was sure that their one small paragraph handed in was not adequate. I tried to explain that if a paper requires three supports, then you have one paragraph for the introduction, three paragraphs for the three supports, and finally the last paragraph for the conclusion. In other words, they needed five paragraphs, not just one small paragraph. After much debate, which caused tempers to rise to near mutiny peak, I conceded that I was wrong and that they should proceed according to their regular format, even if that meant the next fifty minutes was spent trying to make sure everyone did not throw paper airplanes or spitballs!

• • • • • • • • •

The next worst thing that can happen to a substitute teacher is to be in a classroom for three days watching a video movie and, moreover, having to watch a movie that had a poor rating! For example, I substituted in a class where they were to watch the video movie *The Secret Life of Walter Mitty* with Danny Kaye and Virginia Mayo. For all of Danny Kaye's show business talents, Danny Kaye has never appeared in a quality, serious movie other than perhaps a Walt Disney movie for children, nor has Virginia Mayo enjoyed a reputation for artistic achievement. As for *The Secret Life of Walter Mitty*, the short story form does not have enough of a complex, in-depth theme in order to sustain a two-hour movie. I suspect that on a scale of one to ten, the movie would have rated a four in the 1940s and a one or a zero after the 1950s; yet there I was with a class of close to thirty very lively delinquents who were bored beyond endurance and who were determined to rewrite the movie in their version one way or another. I felt like an unsuccessful vaudeville performer on stage who is muttering to himself under his breath, "I'm dying! I'm bombing right here in front of God and everybody!!"

While on the subject of films, I recall a reversal of the above experience with films. I was substituting in vocational agriculture class one day for a class of all boys, and the assignment was to watch two films. One film was on agriculture accidents, and the other one was about soil erosion. One of the morning classes asked if they could come in through the noon hour and watch the film again. I was overjoyed that students actually wanted to contribute part of the noon hour to watching an educational film, so I felt equally obligated to match my enthusiasm with their request. I gladly agreed to donate a half-hour out of my noon hour to open up the room and to show the film for anyone interested in seeing it again. About halfway through the film, when it came time for the tractor accident, they wanted to run the film backwards. So we did. The laughter nearly shook the walls, and I realized that the sole purpose for wanting to see the film again was to be able to see it backwards! Oh, well, I believe in counting our wins rather than our losses, and if students are excited about watching a film, even though it is backwards, I say, "Let's do it!"

• • • • • • • •

The best classes to substitute in are the math classes. Everything is black and white. Usually the instructions are to do problems one to twenty, etc., on pages such and such.

The students most generally know how to work the problems, so it is just a matter of whether there is time enough allotted to do their work. They are busy beavers, thank heavens!

• • • • • • • • •

Once when I was substituting for the computer teacher, he left very detailed instructions with several last words of caution. He instructed me to watch that they do not steal the electrical outlet plugs off the floors and to watch that they do not plug into one another's computer terminals. Well, we were about halfway into the assignment, when I heard one of the Pom-pom girls (with her short miniskirt) say to several of the boys, "Hey, you guys stop that right now." Immediately, my first reaction was to admonish them verbally by saying, "Boys, do not plug into the girls' terminals," but thinking, before saying it, saved me from a great deal of embarrassment. I thought I better become more familiar with computer language before I began intimating things like, "Boys, do not plug into the girls' terminals."

• • • • • • • • •

"I dribbled to my right, and then I dribbled to the left. Then I drove down the court leaving behind first a forward, next a guard, another guard, and suddenly I was all alone thundering toward the basket ready to drive and to stuff the lay-up that would win the game and send us to the playoffs. And then I heard a snap." I headed for my desk and proceeded to take the roll and the class was saying pleadingly, "Well, what happened? What happened?" (They refused to work unless I told them the end of the story). "OK. OK. Where was I? Oh, yes. I heard the snap. I looked to see if my bra strap was hanging below my warm-up, but I finally figured where the snap was coming from."

"Yea, where," they asked.

"It was the ball talking to me just begging me to lay it in for a swish of two points."

"Boo, that was a terrible story."

"I agree, but then so was the ball game."

"Boo's" again.

"Okay, I'll tell you another story. You are to answer all of the questions at the end of the hour or there will be a most unhappy ending to this story ... now get to work!"

"Boos" again.

• • • • • • • • •

There was an expression I coined in the '70s and repeated while substituting in the '80s. It went like this: "We used to hire teachers and hope they could coach. Now we hire coaches and hope they can teach." Amazingly I had that repeated to me, just as if THAT student was the originator of the quote, in the community college where I taught some years later. How the quote evolved was due to the observation of seeing ten coaches teaching and coaching a student body population of about six hundred and fifty. How would it be possible to teach in the daytime, coach in the evening, and hope to attain merit status within the profession? The public screams for merit teaching, but utters not one whisper about offering athletics throughout the year from ages eight on up. Try to convince a parent that his child does not need the winter sports of wrestling and basketball and "conditioning" during the summer months, and you will face an angry, irrational mob. In the first place, I could never understand why it was necessary to have conditioning in the summer time! After all, if youth cannot keep fit through baseball, swimming, tennis, golf and other summer-related activities, I question whether a paid-sponsored activity such as conditioning is contributing to "building character." We pay for what we get, and right now athletics is a viable, strong force within the educational system. Some colleges, though, are beginning to try to turn around the priorities of athletics over academics, and to what degree of success they promote will also determine the course of athletics in our secondary schools.

In one particular high school, there is what is called ALC, or alternative learning center. This is a class for those students who cannot comply with the school rules of behavior and conduct, or students who receive unexcused absences, or students who receive after-school detention and fail to keep the assigned date for detention. These ALC students are segregated from the student body both physically and socially. They are to take a separate noon hour, stay in a small isolated room with a supervisor, and they cannot talk to the other students in the room while they are serving the ALC time. Assignments are sent daily from individual teachers who must okay their work and add additional daily work for each day to five days, depending upon the severity of the punishment.

One day, while substituting for the ALC supervisor (usually a muscular, husky, ex-coach or coach), I met a boy who turned out to be a neighbor of mine down the street from me. We visited during the noon hour on various subjects, and in so doing, I discovered that he, like myself, was a motorcycle fan. I happened to mention that I needed to take my battery out of the cycle now that winter was approaching, but that I was having difficulty getting the bolt of the battery container loosened. He said that he would be glad to take it out for me. He spoke with such a kindness and sincerity that although I was sure my son would help me, too, I accepted his gesture to want to help. Late that afternoon, right on schedule, he knocked on the door and was ready to work. For him the task was not formidable, and there was an expression of satisfaction on his face for him to be able to complete a task so efficiently. While watching him work, I thought about the incongruity of what we teach to prepare a student for higher education in comparison to what a student needs in everyday survival. Here I had just completed my Master's Degree, and yet I could not even take out my motorcycle battery. It took someone from ALC to show the way. As my oldest son (the sympathetic one) says, "Mother, you should not own something you cannot service yourself." (Need I remind him that he never changed his own diapers?) What he fails to understand is that for our generation, basic maintenance was knowing how to cook and sew and take care of our husbands and kids. Let his generation be the caretakers of maintenance.

• • • • • • • •

Do you think students are ever afraid of their teachers

anymore? When I was in grade school, I can remember being terrified of quite a few teachers, and a cousin of mine used to retch if a teacher even looked threatening, but I do not see that happening today.

• • • • • • • • •

"Hello, I am your friendly substitute. This is my diploma, my sorority card, my campfire beads and my motorcycle license. Make no mistake — I am qualified to teach you! Oh, you laugh, do you? Well, someday, you'll regret having laughed at my credentials. Someday I will own this chalk, this ruler, the stapler, and all of the blackboards will be mine and the overhead projector, and you won't be laughing then."

• • • • • • • • •

One time in a middle school, I substituted for a math teacher. He left instructions for us to go to the auditorium to watch a half-hour film along with two or three other math classes from the other grades. When the film was over, we were to return to class in order for them to write a paragraph telling what they liked or disliked about the film. After their written assignment, they were to do two crossword puzzles for extra credit. At the beginning of the second hour (and the second time to repeat the assignment), a boy had not taken his seat by the time of the tardy bell, nor did he hear me tell him several times after the bell had rung to sit down. Actually he was quite busy visiting with his friends in back of him. Finally, I said, "Hey, fella, I said to sit down." We proceeded to go to the film, and from the film we returned to finish the written assignment. As the papers were beginning to be handed in, I collected them in my hand while I made my way around the room "watching." I looked up to see the same kid out of his seat once more and carrying on another lively discussion with other students around him. Since the rows were in close proximity to one another, hardly allowing room for passage, I reached across and tapped him on the head with some papers to get his attention, and again reminded him to sit down. The "tap" must have scared him so that when he did sit down, he rowdily tipped over the desk.

Heeding all the warnings to substitutes to maintain discipline, I sternly said, "All right, that will cost you sixty minutes of detention for being rough on the furniture." I filled out the assertive discipline form, had him sign it and handed him his copy. There was a dead stillness for the rest of the hour. One could only hear breathing in the room.

About two classes later, the principal came up to me and asked what was the "problem" second hour? (Undoubtedly the frightened boy, who likewise happened to be a minister's son, had run to the office telling them that I had hit him.) I said to the principal, "Oh, I didn't realize that there was a "problem." I had this boy, whom I had to tell to sit down four or five times, so I 'tapped' him on the head with some papers to get his attention and obviously I did get his attention because he sat down but knocked over a desk doing so and that was when I gave him the detention slip."

The principal admonished, "Yes, but we can't hit the students in any way. I would rather that you did not do that again."

I apologized and said that I knew at the time that I should not have done that, and it would certainly not happen again. He sympathized, but cautioned me again that rules will not allow hitting in any form. If the conversation had ended right there, we would have mutually agreed on discipline, but he couldn't resist adding that famous one liner, "Well, normally the boy is not any discipline problem."

In other words, below the surface connotation of that remark was the implied belief that the incident was MY fault that he misbehaved. An utterance like this asks of one to buy the logic that since the student had not been any problem yesterday, he will not be any problem tomorrow. Yet, I am saying that on that given day, at that given hour, I determined that the boy created a disturbance. Oh, I am sure that ordinarily the boy was a "model student," and I would have agreed one hundred per cent with the office if they had compromised on the punishment. It is just that I like my word and reputation to be taken seriously, too, and not to be questioned in matters of discipline (especially discipline). By phrasing the question, "What was the problem second hour?" as opposed to "What happened second hour?" the administrator demonstrated a preestablished opinion as to what transpired within the classroom.

I once knew a principal who would ask the teacher's opinion about a complaint from a parent, and when the teacher summarized the problem, the principal would say, "Fine, I'll take care of it. I just wanted to verify from you what action you wanted me to take." Hence, a teacher rarely had to engage in a "hearing" among teacher-parent-and-administrator, but more importantly, the teacher had that vote of confidence which, in turn, caused a reciprocal loyalty and dedication to the "system." I told a fellow colleague in that same middle school about the incident of that day, and his response was, "If we can't hit them, do you suppose we could bite them?"

I harbor no innate hostility toward administrators nor bear animosity toward authority figures. On a one-on-one personable basis, most problems can ultimately be resolved. Why teachers and administrators periodically clash is because the end goals are of opposite poles. Administrators must make money (or at least not lose money), and faculty must be committed to saving souls such as Bertrand Russell once wrote: "Education should be directed toward the reconstruction of human character." To sacrifice to less than saving souls seems neither logical nor honest. Our Kansas dramatist, William Inge, prophetically addressed much of the same dilemma and frustration of many teachers in his play *Bus Stop* of 1955. Dr. Lyman (an ex-college professor) said:

> Every day there would be a meeting of everyone on the entire faculty, with whom the students ever came into any contact, from the President down to the chambermaids, and we would put our collective head together to try to figure out why little Jane or little Mary was not getting out of her classes what she *should.* The suggestion that perhaps she wasn't studying was too simple, and if you implied that she

simply did not have the brains for a college education, you were being undemocratic ... One day I decided I had had enough. I walked blithely into the Dean's office and said, "Sir! I graduated *magna cum laude* from the University of Chicago, I studied at Oxford on a Rhodes Scholarship and returned to take my Ph.D. at Harvard, receiving it with highest honors. I think I have the right to expect my students to try to understand me."

• • • • • • • • •

During my teaching in the early '70s, I remember being called in the principal's office to hear a complaint from a parent about the word "damn" being used in a short story. The material had already been used in the system five years prior to my teaching. That in itself established credibility that the high school ordered the material, stocked the material and obviously endorsed the material into the curriculum. Even if I had emphasized that cuss word, which I never did in any of my classes, the point was that the material represented our school; and, therefore, any complaint should have gone no further than the head office. I always have told students that if I can take out any objectionable words in a story or novel and still have a quality piece of literature, I will teach it, and that includes *Catcher in the Rye*. Before being challenged by a school board or a group of parents, I would ask that first, let me teach the novel to them before making any preconceived, surface judgments without analysis and inquiry and STUDY. We do not have to commit to memory what is written on restroom walls and neither do we need give significance to some ten words out of perhaps one thousand to five thousand words.

The woman kept arguing about the short story in question and prefacing her arguments with, "Oh, honey, those words are all through the story." Finally, I looked at her and said, "Madam, I am neither your honey nor your friend, and what is more I have to go home, go get groceries, fix supper and be ready to sponsor the pom-pom girls at tonight's football game, so I refuse to discuss this any further. Good day."

I do not consider visiting with parents obligatory — I consider it a privilege! If I were in a position to determine classroom policy, I would welcome, perhaps even make mandatory, that parents visit the classrooms and consult teachers about methods and procedures. What I lack tolerance for, though, is fanatical, illogical, petty complaints which detract from the time a teacher could be giving to the more critical needs of ever so many students. If parents and teachers could think of their roles as positive planners, rather than critical analysts, I am sure the students would be the recipients of more individualized guidance.

• • • • • • • •

My oldest son, who also spent a year substituting, said that if he ever wanted anything at school, he always went straight to the secretaries — they incontrovertibly managed the school and kept the system operating smoothly.

I found this to be true. As the secretaries go, so goes the administration. But if you have a secretary acting like work is a drudgery and her duties do not include helping anyone, then nine times out of ten you have a mediocre administration. Answering a telephone, for instance, with a very cheerful, "May I help you?" can set the tone for the entire office.

• • • • • • • •

Prior to the Christmas vacation, I was substituting for an English teacher for the entire week. An announcement came to our room telling students that the student council would appreciate a donation of toys from the student body. These toys were to be wrapped and distributed to various families for $2 a box at the student council Christmas party. Knowing that the President of the Student Council was sitting on the front row of my class, I gingerly began teasing him about the charge of $2 for toys. I goaded him about the point that if the "poor" had the $2 for toys, would they be poor in the first place? He defended the purpose of the $2 charge by explaining that the gesture allowed a family to pay for what they select without feeling the gift was entirely charity. "What does the student council do with the $2 that they collect?" I followed up. "The money will go for paying for the Christmas wrapping," he replied. The next day there was a petition circulated by non-student council members of the student body requesting that the toys be given away to the poor rather than put a price on them. I heard the same arguments in the faculty lounge about how asking a small price for the toys helped needy persons retain their dignity. I silently sat shocked at the logic, but since I was only a visiting faculty member, I, for once, said nothing. On the tip of my tongue I wanted to ask, how do you value human dignity? Is it worth a dollar? Two dollars? Who determines what pride and dignity are worth?

• • • • • • • •

So far, I have substituted in all of the teaching fields except gym. I have been to shop, vocational agriculture, art, physics, Latin, Spanish, French, Debate, Computer, Drama and, oh, yes, English. The first time I went to substitute in vocational agriculture, I did not know the teacher. It so happened that he was a relatively new teacher to the system, and he happened to be very, very young — none of this I knew at the time. When I went into the room early in the morning to get myself organized for the day, I saw two "students" sitting at a desk. I began looking around for my material and trying the doors to the teacher's office, and every time I was trying to locate something, this one "student" kept volunteering information to me about where to find things and what I was to do. I thought to myself, "Oh, oh, I've got a know-it-all-kid trying to tell me what to do. I decided that if he persisted in butting in, I would have to show the kid who was boss around there — after all, I was the one with the keys. I had the authority! Finally, he spoke up, "Thank you for taking my classes while I go to the Ag convention today. Here are the assignments for today." I stood there with my mouth wide open, barely able to acknowledge his instructions. I humbly accepted his help and confessed to him that I thought he was a student. Apparently he was accustomed to the case of mistaken identity because he good-naturedly assured me that the mistaken identity happened all of the time.

I admire people who can make one feel comfortable when one has made a mistake. Some people USE one's mistakes to prop up their own inadequacies. This kind of behavior is evident when some people drive. Many drivers give others the horn when they make a mistake, while others accept what cannot be undone. In fact, honking at someone can contribute to additional mistakes since one might be looking around to see who was honking and whether it was for the previous mistake or some other impending danger one failed to see.

• • • • • • • • •

Personally, I rather like to go for job interviews. Seldom does anyone ask a teacher what he or she thinks about education that, frankly, I welcome the opportunity for dialectic discourse on education. All I need to set me off is for someone to say, "What do you think about education?" Of course, in a job interview situation, one always gambles on whether one should be assertive or controlled, liberal or conservative, philosophical or practical, or ask questions or give answers. The best interview I felt that I ever had was with a panel of five. Instead of the usual questions on procedure, benefits and requirements, their questions revolved around philosophical questions along the lines of: How would I handle discipline? What materials do I feel comfortable teaching? Was I a team teacher? What was my grading philosophy? What are my methods of teaching? Then one woman, who was chairwoman of the English Department, asked me what I thought about teaching foreign students? Since she knew I had taught several summers at a community college teaching American Literature for foreign student classes, she guided the topic of conversation in that direction. Particularly she queried me on the subject of cheating and what I thought about the prevalent use of cheating on tests by foreign students. I was ready for the question, and I knew by looking at her facial expression and the way that she broached the subject, that she had a strong opinion on the subject already. So did I. The foreign students at the community college during the late '60s drove the teachers insane with their innate proclivity to cheat on the exams. They tended to be "thieves of Baghdad," I admitted, but I wondered what temptations and pressures we would succumb to if we were in their country and we could not adequately understand the material that was necessary to master in order to keep pace with the native students. Anyway, I proceeded to answer her question. "First of all," I informed the panel, "I think we have to take into consideration the fact that foreign students do NOT consider cheating on exams morally wrong in their culture. Therefore, it is very difficult to convince a student that it is wrong to cheat when ninety-nine to one hundred per cent practice cheating daily. You have to approach cheating where it hurts the most — the pocketbook — or in other words, the grades." She looked at me dubiously as if I were the foreign object of the moment. I continued more in depth on the subject, "When I taught American Literature for foreign students, I finally adopted a code whereby if anyone talked during a test, I would automatically drop their score one grade lower on his test score. Even if he were only asking for a pencil, still I gave one grade deduction for the individual asking the question and one grade lower for the other individual who would be unfortunate enough to respond. That was the only procedure that I found to be to be successful in any extent in the prevention of cheating on tests. Where I tried several other measures such as confiscating the individual's test paper if he talked, I was not as successful doing that as the method of the grade penalty." The chairwoman, without benefit of exposure to the problem, looked skeptical to the means one would have to cope with in translating and transmitting material to a diverse type of learner.

Aside from the ever-present cheating, I found foreign students extremely rewarding to teach. For one thing, they are appreciative of education, and they value it not only as a means for staying out of one Mideast crisis after another, but also as a means of ambitious advancement. Also, the foreign students revere the mother-image type of teacher and grant her all of the respect and attention that they would accord their own mothers. A friend of mine had a daughter teaching composition to foreign students in Tulsa University, but because this young married teacher was pregnant and "belonged in the home," as they paraphrased their cultural mores, she was all but boycotted from the classroom. The last I knew she had bitterly resigned from that position to accept any type of work which did not involve foreign students. But I think what I enjoyed the most in teaching foreign students was the overwhelming challenge of presenting material that they could grasp and comprehend, and certainly with their innate intelligence, coupled with a well-founded background in the academics, the teaching experience often transcended the expectations of American education.

All things considered, I thoroughly enjoyed my interview, and I sensed by the facial reactions of at least four out of the five panel that they liked what they heard. I inwardly knew that I was in command of the interview and that the occasion was one of those times when the words and ideas harmoniously blended. Several days later, I received a letter from the high school principal informing me:

Dear Amy:

We have made a selection for the English position of Junior Class English teacher. At the June 7th Board of Education meeting we will recommend Mary Rogers to fill the English vacancy created by the resignation of Shirley Johnson.

Seldom have we had such a difficult time making a selection since we had such an outstanding field of candidates.

I appreciated the super interview we had and I thank you for your time and interest.

Sincerely,

(Ironically, I could not read his illegible handwriting but, of course, I knew the signature of the acting principal.)

Stan says there are two kinds of interviews — those given by the bad guys and those given by the regulars (or the nice guys). He, too (with his double Masters Degree in both English and Spanish and a Ph.D. degree also), has been in situations where he had to decide whether to give the interviewer what he wanted to hear or give the interviewer what he needed to hear! According to Stan, an example of how a mediocre principal conducts an interview is to say: "Can you promise to get your students through the book by the end of the year?" This typifies an administrator locked into teaching "by the book," and he could have the best teacher in the state sitting before him, but he would give finishing the book by the end of the year the most important priority of teaching. I happen to be very frightened of administrators who rank keeping the halls free of traffic as one of the prime concerns in education. That thought is akin to saying tidy rooms and tidy halls produce tidy students, and I suppose to an extent that is most correct, but I also believe the obsessiveness of an administrator produces tidy minds which culminate into tiny minds. As Ralph Waldo Emerson wrote: "A foolish consistency is the hobgoblin of little minds." Emerson also proved that an individual could have a strong foundation of religion and be of resolute character and still adopt self-reliance.

During one interview, recalled by Stan, was when a principal wanted to know if he (Stan) could work with an all-woman English faculty? Stan said that he did not know whether to laugh or be insulted, for as he mused the question, he reminded himself that there were very few people in the '80s who denied a woman's presence in the work force.

Another interview I had took place in Kansas City at one of the community colleges. The market in the mid '80s was so deflated for English teachers that I found myself driving around checking out all possible leads to future openings. That was the case when I began reading the "Help Wanted" section of the *Kansas City Star* and began also checking out job possibilities before they were even advertised as jobs.

Consequently, I assumed the role of an eager beaver willing to investigate all job possibilities. Actually just any job selection was not altogether accurate. I had eliminated those jobs requiring coaching or sponsoring pom-pom or cheerleading. I felt that I had been that route before back in the '70s; and besides, healthwise, I was positive that I could not be effective in my teaching by riding a bus once a week and taking tickets at a game another night of the week and yet be expected to grade English themes late at night.

I doubted whether the Kansas City interview would be productive, but I had promised a friend to explore as many avenues of employment as possible. He arranged, therefore, an interview with the Director of the Placement Bureau, at her convenience. That meant by the time I managed to be admitted to her office, several hours had elapsed, and I had had time to reflect upon the interview and the college. When the secretary said that the director would see me now, I harbored considerable doubts about teaching in the big city, and after about fifteen minutes of visiting with the busy executive, I was convinced that I was not destined for the pressures and hassles or urban competition. She helped me with that decision with indefatigable emphasis on the information that their community college was a very prestigious college and that they recruited nationwide for the best of teachers. She paused a moment to let that bit of name-dropping to register with my perception, and I likewise paused to digest what was undoubtedly a streamline snobbish sales pitch designed to impress everyone from the East Coast to the West Coast. I retaliated by saying that I can appreciate the fact that they recruit nationwide, but no matter how many degrees a teacher had or from what university, good teaching depends upon whether the teacher can draw students to her class and keep them there, and that I can do! She thanked me and suggested I fill out an application form with her secretary for any opening in the future. I said "thank you," walked out, and kept walking right past the application desk.

• • • • • • • •

To pass the tedium of the time, I sent the following note to a student in one of the English classes I was substituting in at the local high school:

> Word has come to my office (by way of a beautiful, intelligent source) that you were seen Thursday morning, April 5th, out to Wal-Marts instead of being at the community college or high school studying. I consider this a gross negligence of duty to our beloved high school, so I am giving you sixty minutes of detention to be served by April 9th. Be there! Also I am dropping your 4.0 grade-point average to a 3.9. How do you like them apples?
>
> Signed,
> Your substitute principal

The student receiving this note had a wonderful sense of humor and was instigating ever so many "digs" at me throughout the substituting tour of duty, thus making the hours more enjoyable and the days more bearable. When the day arrives that I do not have fun with teaching, I won't teach. I did worry about saying "them apples" instead of those apples, but an old expression from the '50s just naturally slipped out, and since it was a noticeable grammatical slip, I was sure she would note that it was a "slang expression."

• • • • • • • • •

Oh, no, I am practically choking this kid. What on earth possessed me to do such a thing. I looked at my hand latched on to his blond lock of hair, and I could not believe that I was pulling on it as one would a rope on a runaway dog. How could I do such a thing! Perhaps I was unduly influenced by the coaches whom I had seen muscle a few of the recalcitrants, and do so quite successfully. At times a woman envies the command a heavy hand places upon possible delinquents, but in reality, I should have realized that I could never assume that role. I have that mother-me-softly type of face which does not threaten nor scare the hardest of hearts. Besides, who can predict that the "mothering" can save as many souls as the "heavy hands?"

• • • • • • • • •

Another time I was substituting in the computer class there was a student whom I was acquainted with in a prior confrontational episode on a previous day. When I had substituted in a history class, for instance, she posed a considerable giggly disturbance, and I found it necessary to cite her as a detention candidate. Since that time, we had become acquainted and even enjoyed a friendly conversation from time to time. On the day of the computer class, most of the students immediately went to their computers and proceeded with their assignments. A few of the students worked at their desks and waited to share a computer since they were four or five computers short for the class to use at the same time. This particular girl, however, neither worked at a computer nor worked at her desk, but instead, somewhat drifted about the room, first disturbing one student after another. After what I considered ample time to work off her restlessness, I finally asked her to please go to her desk and find SOMETHING to do. She cooperated with that dictum, but after about ten minutes, when it was obvious that several students at their desks were oblivious to her conversation, and certainly the "computees" were too busy for her, she looked up at me wistfully and almost pitifully and said, "Ms. Talbott, will you come here, please?" When I went to her desk at the back of the room, I said, "Cheryl, what did you want?" She looked up at me with sad eyes and said, "Will you sit down with me and visit for awhile? I just want someone to talk to." I answered, "Sure, Cheryl, let's gossip for a bit." That day, I felt that I more nearly earned my pay than other previous days, and I hoped that Cheryl enjoyed our visit, too.

• • • • • • • • •

Well, the school year is finished, and as three English positions opened up in the middle school in the spring, I got another one of those letters saying, "We regret to inform you that we will be recommending another candidate for the position for which you applied. Thank you for your time and effort." I do wish that they would have added, "Thank you also for spending a portion of your savings each month in order to pay the bills while substituting for our district."

It seems that I am in an era where age and experience are not virtues, but they are vices in educational systems which thrive in hiring those "straight out of college." Experienced teachers are no longer in demand nor a "premium" in a society which values individual strength and character as a commodity to be bought or bargained for at the cheapest price.

What will I do next? Where will I go? I will worry about it tomorrow, and for today, I will get on my motorcycle and ride out on the country roads. You see, when I am out on the cycle, riding in the wind, with the sun tanning my face, I transcend the complexity of everyday existence, and there euphorically comes to me from within my soul, the melody of a song that I especially enjoy. I never know what the tune will be, but I do know that I begin singing, and I am happy once again. A person who sings on the cycle can't be all bad, right?

• • • • • • • •
The End
• • • • • • • •

EPILOGUE

Sandra L. Dudley went on to become a teacher at Fort Scott Community College from 1985 to 2000. She replaced the mentor who had influenced her English aspirations. After retirement in 2000, she was elected to the college Board of Trustees from 2000-2004.

During the time teaching at Fort Scott Community College, she merited the following awards:

(1) Semifinalist in the 1994 edition of poetry in *Echoes of Yesterday* in the 1994 National Library of Poetry

(2) Teacher Recognition Award 1995-96 from the University of Kansas College of Liberal Arts and Sciences

(3) Teacher Recognition Award 1996-97 from the University of Kansas College of Liberal Arts and Sciences

(4s) Biography published in the Fifth Edition of *Who's Who Among Teachers,* 1998

(5) NISOD Excellence Award Recipient, 1998.